JN441578

Discussion Textbook for Intermediate and Advanced Students

# EXPRESS YOURSELF DIRECTLY 1

Written by LIS KOREA Editorial Staff & Duane Vorhees

# Introduction

**LIS KOREA** is unique among publishers. It is the only one in the world that is devoted solely to developing its readers' ability to think in a foreign language rather than merely communicate in it.

Most second-language instruction manuals assume that there is always just one answer to every problem, and that students can be programmed to provide precisely that answer. In the real world, alas, neither assumption has much validity. Everyone sees a situation differently and responds to it individually. It is this organic approach to communication that LIS Korea always promotes rather than basic skills such as grammar and punctuation.

The newest production of LIS Korea, EXPRESS YOURSELF DIRECTLY, follows the basic philosophy of EXPRESS YOURSELF but presents it in an entirely new and different way by relying far less on text examples as potential models and instead presenting a vast number of illustrations carefully designed to provoke thought, encourage discussion, and assert individual attitudes. It is intended to be a hands-on, interactive, and provocative but humorously engaging mentor. It is sure to entertain and inform all users, teachers and students alike.

# Contents

# Does Your Car Mean More Than Just a Driving Machine?

## Pictures Talk

1

Q1) What is your favorite car? Why?

Q2) Are you willing to buy an imported car if it is affordable? What do you think about buying a used car?

Q1) Have you ever been in a traffic accident? Describe what happened.

Q2) It has become common practice for drivers to be hospitalized when they are involved in ANY accident, even if they are not hurt. What do you think about patients who go to the hospital even though they are not seriously injured?

Q1) When you are stuck in a traffic jam, do you get nervous? What do you do in such a case?

Q2) How can traffic jams be avoided?

Q1) Why is speeding dangerous?

Q2) On an expressway, how fast do you usually drive? What is the fastest you've ever driven?

An automobile is a means of transportation, of course. But it is so much more than that. It is an expression of personality — do you drive a cute, efficient, little compact? — an SUV? — a stretch limo? What does that say about you? It is also a status symbol; only people who are well-off can drive an expensive new car — and get a new one every year!

5

Q1) Everybody knows driving drunk is dangerous, but many still do it. Can you explain why?

Q2) What do you think is the proper punishment for DWI (driving while intoxicated)?

6

Q1) Do you think gas prices are too high? How can people save gas?

Q2) Have you ever considered using a motorcycle or bicycle instead of a car to save money?

7

Q1) Name some common distractions for ordinary drivers. How dangerous are they?

Q2) Some drivers and passengers throw cigarette butts and empty soda cans on the road. What do you think about their behavior?

8

Q1) Motorcyclists are not allowed on the expressways. Is that necessary or fair? What do you think?

Q2) If they were permitted, what do you think would happen?

# Express Yourself Directly

1. Name some common traffic rules average drivers often break? For violators, do you think the punishment fits the wrongdoing?
2. How many cars does your family need? Who decides which vehicle to buy?
3. Who do you think drives better, men or women?
4. Talk about your priorities when buying a car.
5. Traffic fatalities are on the rise. Is your life insured? Why or why not?
6. Would you be willing to give up your car if mass transit were convenient enough?
7. Do you think a car represents the owner's social and financial status? Why or why not?
8. Talk about the ways you think cars will develop in the future.

# Let's Talk Funny

## What's in a Name?

**Racer**: I love my sports car!

**Mortician**: Why?

**Racer**: Because in my profession, a sports car means speed and power.

**Mortician**: That's interesting. In my profession, S-P-OR-T-S car means Speed, Power, OR Tragic Suicide.

## Questions

(1) How do the two people view sports cars differently?

(2) Can you think of any examples of people seeing some object very differently, depending on their situation? (For example, a wedding ring from the perspectives of a jeweler and a bride)

# What Does It Mean?

1

Many people have trouble with their new car. The engine won't start but the payments won't stop.

Nothing depreciates a car faster than having a neighbor buy a newer one.

The best car-safety device is a rearview mirror with a cop in it.

Anyone driving slower than you is an idiot, and anyone going faster than you is a maniac.

Teenagers think they know all about driving a car once they learn where the horn is located.

These expressions are related to the topics in this chapter. It will be good speaking practice to let students explain what these sentences mean in their own words in English.

6

It's better to crash into a nap than nap into a crash.

7

The biggest need in auto society is the recall of a few million defective drivers.

8

It takes 8,460 bolts to assemble an automobile, and just one nut to scatter it all over the road.

9

By the time a man can afford to buy one of those little sports cars, he's too fat to get into it.

10

If GM had kept up with technology like the computer industry has, we would all be driving $25 cars that get 1,000 MPG.

1

This one's so cute, Honey. And it's only a few thousand more.

I think this cheap one is even cuter.

2

You rear-ended me. It's all your fault!

I wouldn't have rear-ended you if you hadn't backed into me at full speed.

10

The view along this road is magnificent! And these hairpin curves are exciting.

I think another fool is coming to populate my cemetery.

Think of these cartoons as scenes in a movie. The dialog has been scripted. Now we need actors to play the parts.

9

My new water-powered car is a great idea, especially since no one drinks tap water anymore.

A solar-powered car is wonderful except at night.

My air-powered car solves all the problems! But I need a pump that uses gas or solar power.

— Did you see that "No motorcycle" sign?
— What sign? You must have misread it.
— I guess so. Not allowing our bike on the expressway makes no sense at all.

3

4

## S·Y·N·O·P·S·I·S

These are the pictures you've seen in this chapter. It will be good speaking practice for you to talk about these pictures once again. Your teacher will ask you "What are they doing?" or "What does this picture mean?" or some other question. You can give a straight answer or you can use your imagination. The purpose is to allow free conversation; there is no "right" answer.

S·Y·N·O·P·S·I·S

5

I won't let you drive in your condition. It's not safe!

Get out of the way. You know I'm too drunk to walk.

6

7

11

I know it's expensive to fix the starter. But my legs are killing me.

Can you push a little faster, Dear? I'm late to work.

12

How do you like my new car? I got a great deal on it!

Why do I bother washing my old car? No matter how hard I work, it still looks old.

20

I just hope my car's computer doesn't CRASH.

Think of these cartoons as scenes in a movie. The dialog has been scripted. Now we need actors to play the parts.

19

Now I understand why a sedan is also a rich man's status symbol.

18

Studies have shown that the most dangerous part is the nut behind the wheel.

13

Uh-oh, I left my money at home. I hope this police officer accepts credit cards.

14

I know that the speed limit is always based on a good reason, so I always obey it.

I never pay attention to speed limits — they're just somebody's imaginary numbers.

I think the speed limit is too high. This road is still dangerous.

## S · Y · N · O · P · S · I · S

These are the pictures you've seen in this chapter. It will be good speaking practice for you to talk about these pictures once again. Your teacher will ask you "What are they doing?" or "What does this picture mean?" or some other question. You can give a straight answer or you can use your imagination. The purpose is to allow free conversation; there is no "right" answer.

S · Y · N · O · P · S · I · S

S · Y · N · O · P · S · I · S

15

Crossing the street is dangerous enough, but do we also have to be subjected to noise pollution?

There is nothing difficult about driving a car. You just need one hand on the horn and one foot on the accelerator.

17

Don't look now, but I think God is getting ready to recall US.

16

Times have changed. Nowadays, "Rush hour" means "siesta time."

# Lame Excuses!

## Pictures Talk

Q1) What are the most common excuses for not exercising?

Q2) Do you believe you can stay fit without doing any exercise? How? Do you know any simple, light exercise people can do any place and any time?

Q1) What excuses do husbands use for coming home late and drunk?

Q2) What excuses do wives provide if their hubbies complain about a poor meal?

Q1) How do drunk drivers excuse their actions?

Q2) Why are there still a lot of drunk drivers on the road?

Q1) When drivers are stopped by cops for breaking traffic laws, what excuses do they make?

Q2) Do you think there are any excuses that might persuade a cop not to give you a ticket?

Sometimes accidents happen; the unexpected is always a possibility; and even highly unlikely events may occur from time to time. So it may be the case that we are unavoidably late or that we inadvertently break a promise or violate a trust. At such times, all we can do is explain the circumstances and hope to be forgiven. But most of the time, being human, we simply make a mistake and then try to justify our behavior with a silly or stupid "lame" excuse.

5

Q1) Dieters often fail to lose weight permanently. What are their excuses for failure?

Q2) Most unsuccessful dieters try again and again. Why?

6

Q1) How do the rich justify not helping the poor?

Q2) What are the excuses of poor people for their condition?

7

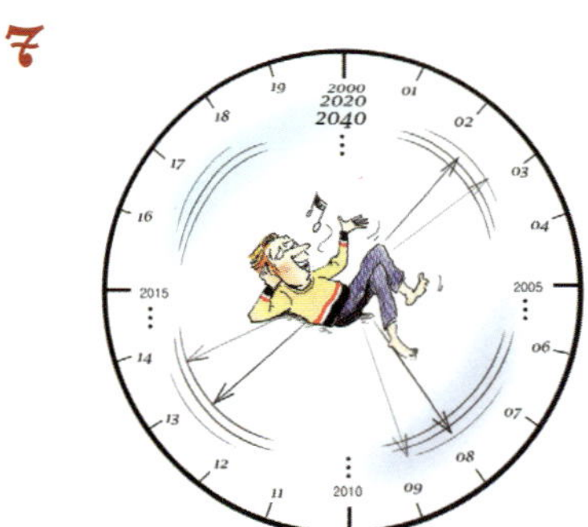

Q1) What excuses do people make who have failed to keep their new year's resolutions?

Q2) Despite previous failures, people still make resolutions in the new year. Why?

8

Q1) What reasons do bosses give for not raising workers' salaries?

Q2) What do workers say when they are asked about coming to work late?

**What excuses do these people commonly make?**

1. Tax evaders
2. Smokers who can't quit
3. Deadbeats
4. Hit-and-run drivers
5. People who regularly buy lottery tickets
6. People who don't answer their phone calls and don't call back
7. Divorcees
8. People who save no money
9. Gold diggers
10. Teachers who spank students
11. Governments that raise taxes but still face stiff inflation

The world's vices are what keep the world in motion. But they are a very fragile base.

# Let's Talk Funny

## ABSENT WITHOUT LEAVE

**Boss**: Why didn't you come to work yesterday?

**Employee**: Sorry, I was in bed all day long with a terrible cold.

**Boss**: You didn't answer my call or even call me back!

**Employee**: I was too sick to get out of bed until this morning.

**Boss**: I can always tell when you are lying. Why do you keep making up these ridiculous stories?

**Employee**: Because any excuse is BETTER THAN NONE.

## Questions

(1) Can you explain why people try to make excuses, even clumsy ones?

(2) What's the difference between a lame excuse and a lie?

# What Does It Mean?

1

Never ruin an apology with an excuse.

2

The only man who is really free is the one who can turn down an invitation to dinner without needing to give an excuse.

3

It is soon going to be too hot to do the job that was too cold to do last winter.

4

The person who really wants to do something finds a way; the other person finds an excuse.

5

Maybe you don't like your job, or maybe you didn't get enough sleep; well, nobody likes his job, and nobody gets enough sleep. Maybe you just had the worst day of your life, but you know there's no escape, there's no excuse, so just suck it up and be nice.

These expressions are related to the topics in this chapter. It will be good speaking practice to let students explain what these sentences mean in their own words in English.

6

The real man is the one who finds excuses for others but never for himself.

7

A flimsy excuse is one that your wife can see through.

8

I attribute my success to this:
I never gave or took an excuse.

9

Not managing your time well and making excuses are two bad habits. But don't put them together by claiming you "don't have the time."

Nothing is impossible; everywhere has a way to get there, and if we have sufficient will we will always find sufficient means. It is merely an excuse that we say something is impossible.

Think of these cartoons as scenes in a movie. The dialog has been scripted. Now we need actors to play the parts.

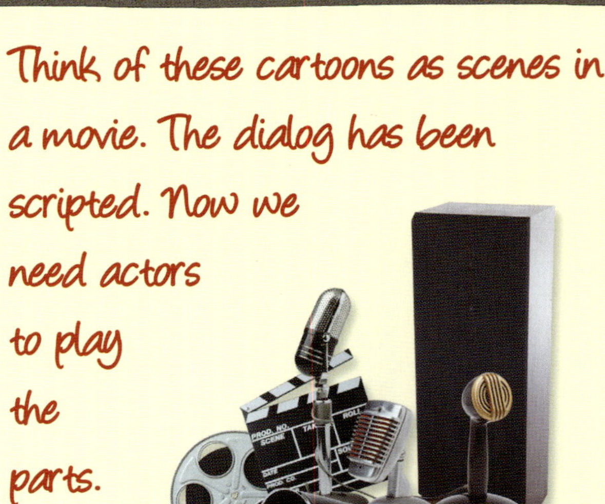

3

A hundred years ago, the horse would take its sleeping master home from the tavern. Nowadays, we let the empty bottles drive.

4

— Let me guess. You have a medical emergency so you are in a hurry. You didn't realize you were speeding and promise to be more careful in the future. Your accelerator was stuck and you couldn't slow down.

— Are you a mind-reader?

— No, but I always get the same set of excuses. Do you have a new one to add to my list, or should I just write the ticket now?

## S·Y·N·O·P·S·I·S

These are the pictures you've seen in this chapter. It will be good speaking practice for you to talk about these pictures once again. Your teacher will ask you "What are they doing?" or "What does this picture mean?" or some other question. You can give a straight answer or you can use your imagination. The purpose is to allow free conversation; there is no "right" answer.

S·Y·N·O·P·S·I·S

5

If I lose just two kilograms a month, in twenty years I will need a scale with negative numbers.

6

Oh! I am burdened down with the weight of my vast wealth. I wish I were free of it!

Let us help you separate yourself from some of your money.

There is nothing harder than getting money from a rich man.

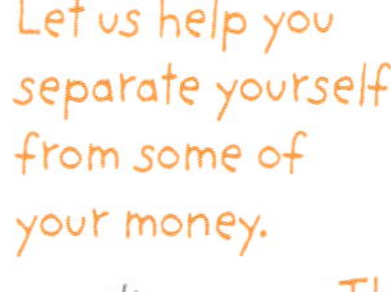

If I had my way, I would leave him alone and just take the money.

What's he complaining about? The rest of us are already free — we aren't worth anything.

7

My New Year's Resolution this year is to break all my resolutions even sooner than I did last year.

11

— I'm so sorry. I didn't mean to say you're fickle.
— That's okay. I forgive you.
— I really meant to say that you should make up your mind.
— Then I guess you're not forgiven after all.
— Then, maybe "fickle" is the right word after all.

12

It's time to cut off the chains that bind me so I can be free to do whatever I like. But maybe this ax is not sharp enough......

20

I don't need two wheels, if one wheel will do.

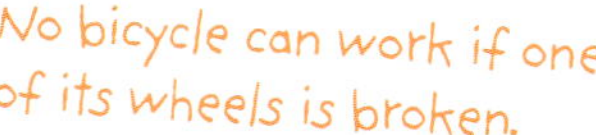

No bicycle can work if one of its wheels is broken.

Think of these cartoons as scenes in a movie. The dialog has been scripted. Now we need actors to play the parts.

19

How do you get so much done in just 24 hours? Just thinking about it makes me exhausted.

18

I didn't read the liar's book that said, "It was never my fault."

**13**

I wish I had some firewood. It's COLD!

It's too hot to cut down this tree. It's the only shade I've got.

**14**

I can do anything if I set my mind to it, but it's not always easy.

I could do it if I wanted to, but life is always easy when someone else does the work.

## S·Y·N·O·P·S·I·S

These are the pictures you've seen in this chapter. It will be good speaking practice for you to talk about these pictures once again. Your teacher will ask you "What are they doing?" or "What does this picture mean?" or some other question. You can give a straight answer or you can use your imagination. The purpose is to allow free conversation; there is no "right" answer.

S·Y·N·O·P·S·I·S

S·Y·N·O·P·S·I·S

**15**

I'm not going to give anyone the satisfaction of knowing how miserable I am.

This fellow seems happy, even though I'm not. So why should I ruin his day by being a grouch?

**16**

I might not be able to hold this gang off by myself, but I'll do the best I can.

If only we had a gun, we could help you out.

Gee, if all of those guys would stand together, they would outnumber us and we wouldn't have a chance.

**17**

The inconsistency in my story was so small I never thought you would see it.

No matter how small your lie is, I can always find a bigger magnifying glass.

# Issue 03 Family Dynamics

## Pictures Talk

1

Q1) Do your family members communicate well with each other?

Q2) If there are problems in communication among your family members, who are the main culprits? Why?

Q1) What are some of the rules in your family?

Q2) Are they well observed? Why or why not?

Q1) Does your extended family often get together?

Q2) What do you do? Who foots the bill?

Q1) How does your family divvy up household chores?

Q2) Is everyone satisfied with the way they are divided up? Why or why not?

All human society is shaped by family structure, but the form the structure takes varies widely. Modern cultures usually regard the nuclear family (parents and children) as ideal, but this ideal family is actually rather rare in modern society, due to high divorce rates and single-parent homes. But any family — nuclear, extended, tribal, polygamous, or same-sex — is composed of individuals with their own wants, needs, and personalities, so it is always difficult (though necessary) to maintain stable and productive relationships within the family.

5

Q1) Do you know how to be a good parent and a good child?

Q2) Which role is more difficult?

Q1) Do you think TVs and computers encourage or discourage family cohesion? Why?

Q2) Can your family go for a week without using a TV or computer? Who is the least likely to be able to do so?

Q1) People generally think a double-income family is better off and happier than a single-income one. Do you agree?

Q2) Do you think moms should stay at home and be full-time housekeepers for the sake of their kids? Why or why not?

Q1) What usually causes married couples to become estranged?

Q2) What are some things that make parents and kids distant from each other?

# Express Yourself Directly

1. Is your family happy?
2. Your "family" can also mean your distant relatives and in-laws. Do you accept them as family?
3. Talk about the good things and bad things that happen when you interact with your relatives.
4. Do you consider your spouse's family as your own? Why or why not?
5. What do you think about three-generation families?
6. What about your neighbors — do you get along well with them? Why or why not?

## The Also-Ran Speaks

**Man**: I'm angry about the way people think about second place in sports.

**Woman**: What do you mean?

**Man**: Let me explain. In professional golf, the second-place person doesn't get any attention at all — and even silver medalists in the Olympic Games are ignored.

**Woman**: Everybody takes that for granted. Why does it upset you?

**Man**: Well, I'm the SECOND BOSS in my family and nobody pays me any attention either!

## Questions

(1) Who is the boss in your family? Who do you think should be?

(2) These days, kids seem to rule the roost in some families. What do you think about that situation?

# What Does It Mean?

1

No matter what you've done for yourself, if you can't look back on having given loving attention to your family, what have you really accomplished?

2

Within the family, any problem, big or small, starts with bad communication: Someone isn't listening.

3

Home is the place where boys and girls first learn to limit their own desires, abide by rules, and consider the rights and needs of others.

The trouble with some families is that they have sedan tastes and compact incomes.

A family consists of a husband who gets an idea, kids who say it can't be done, and a wife who goes and does it.

These expressions are related to the topics in this chapter. It will be good speaking practice to let students explain what these sentences mean in their own words in English.

6

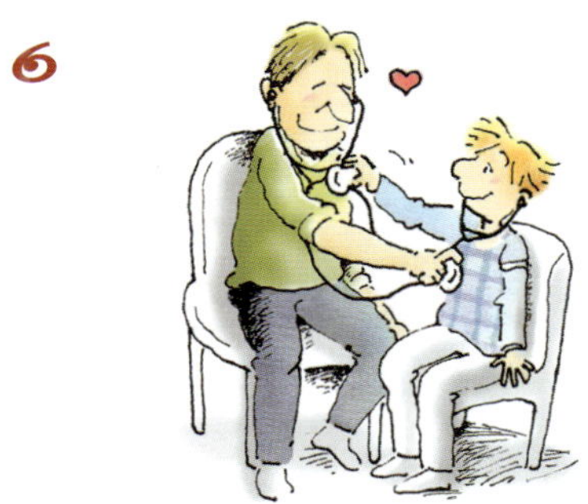

It is not flesh and blood, it is the heart, which makes us fathers and sons.

7

Everyone should have kids. They are the greatest joy in the world. But they are also terrorists. You'll realize this as soon as they're born and they start to break you by using sleep deprivation.

8

A son is a son till he takes him a wife, a daughter is a daughter all of her life.

9

Every father should remember that one day his son will follow his example instead of his advice.

10

If you were about to die and only had one phone call you could make, who would you call and what would you say?

1

Oh, were you speaking to me?

Don't you ever pay any attention to anybody?

Yap! Yap! Yap! I've got issues I want to discuss. Yap! Yap! Yap!

2

Thank God, they don't have any cooking rules in this house. Posting all those notes is so unattractive.

10

I'd like to thank my family for making this possible.......

I'm glad I could do my part for the family's success.

Traditionally, the number-two spot is the clean-up position.

We don't get enough credit for all of our hard work.

Think of these cartoons as scenes in a movie. The dialog has been scripted. Now we need actors to play the parts.

9

Being together gives us much strength and happiness.

All these people next door make too much noise! I wish they would invite me over.

At least you have your loyal dog to keep you company. By the way, where's my bone?

8

Control your temper!

That brat makes me so mad!

What's he so mad about? All I did was put itching powder in his shaving cream.

3

4

# S · Y · N · O · P · S · I · S

These are the pictures you've seen in this chapter. It will be good speaking practice for you to talk about these pictures once again. Your teacher will ask you "What are they doing?" or "What does this picture mean?" or some other question. You can give a straight answer or you can use your imagination. The purpose is to allow free conversation; there is no "right" answer.

S · Y · N · O · P · S · I · S

5

7

6

11

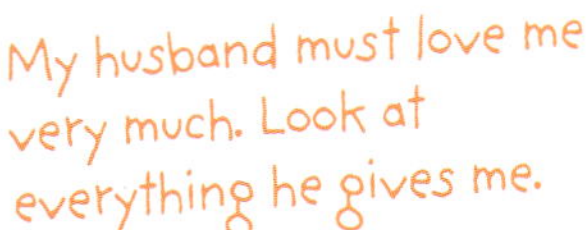

My husband must love me very much. Look at everything he gives me.

It seems that no matter how generous I am, my wife always wants more.

12

– I'm tired of listening to you complain about money all the time. Let's change the subject!
– Who's talking about money? I was complaining about your lack of attention.
– You never listen to me!

20

– I'm dying! Can you grant me one last request?
– You know you can depend on me always. What can I do for you?
– Bring me a triple burger.
– With cheese?
– Yes! And hurry!
– Anything else before you go?
– Hold the mayo.

Think of these cartoons as scenes in a movie. The dialog has been scripted. Now we need actors to play the parts.

19

I want to help my son. Why won't he take my advice?

I want to be like my dad in every way. (But I hope he doesn't go bald.)

18

New name, but still your daughter.

Same name, but on my own now.

13

If you follow these 1,023 simple rules, you will grow up to be responsible adults.

You must memorize and recite them every day.

I wish you hadn't got them that Power Point for their anniversary.

When they get to #500, wake me up. Then you can take your turn to sleep through the last half.

14

It takes a lot of work to keep a car on the road. I need to have this big car, but gas is too expensive.

My compact is easy to drive, easy to park, and easy on the pocket book.

S·Y·N·O·P·S·I·S

These are the pictures you've seen in this chapter. It will be good speaking practice for you to talk about these pictures once again. Your teacher will ask you "What are they doing?" or "What does this picture mean?" or some other question. You can give a straight answer or you can use your imagination. The purpose is to allow free conversation; there is no "right" answer.

S·Y·N·O·P·S·I·S

15

There's a bear! Somebody should call the police!

Will you guys relax? I've already called the cops. They're on their way.

We're doomed! That bear's going to eat us!

Why is everyone so upset? I just wanted to ask directions.

17

I need a break. You two torture her for a while.

I'll bang my drum and "sing" as loud as I can.

I'll make her clean up after me again and again. That'll drive her crazy.

I wish I could get a good night's sleep, just once!

16

I'm not your biological father, but I love you just the same.

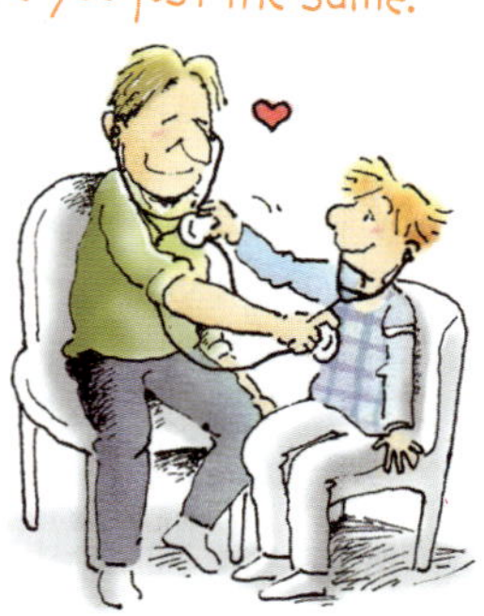

Even if you're not my real dad, no one could ever be a better father to me.

# Issue 04 Ways to Better Health

## Pictures Talk

1

Q1) Which is more important, physical or mental health?

Q2) How can determination promote our own mental health?

2

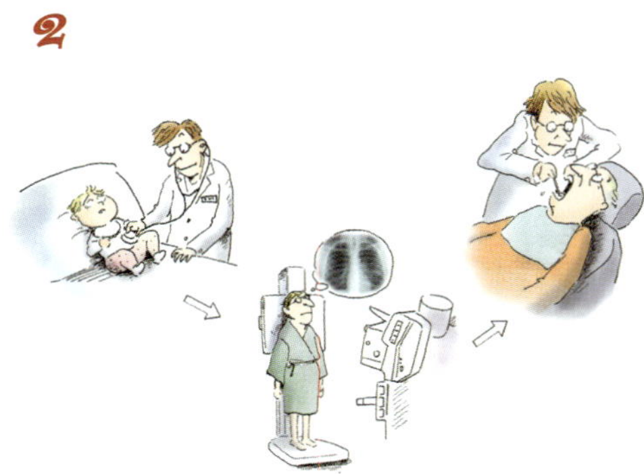

Q1) Prevention is the best medicine. How often do you get a medical checkup?

Q2) Some people don't get regular checkups. Why not?

3

Q1) The cold is one of the most common diseases. When you get one, do you rush to a doctor or just relax and take it easy? Or do you just ignore it and act like you don't have one?

Q2) What do you do to keep from catching a cold?

4

Q1) Do you sleep soundly? Some people don't sleep well. Why not?

Q2) If your spouse snored every night, what would you do?

More than intelligence, wealth, race, status, nationality, occupation, gender, ideology, creed, or education, health seems to be the most important determinant of happiness and success. It is also the least predictable. Bad health consumes resources and energy from other tasks, while good health enables people to focus on other things beyond themselves. Rich people who are very sick are willing to trade their wealth for an end to illness, but not even the poorest person would accept a fortune in exchange for extremely bad health.

Q1) Do you take vitamin pills regularly? Why or why not?

Q2) What do you do to improve your health?

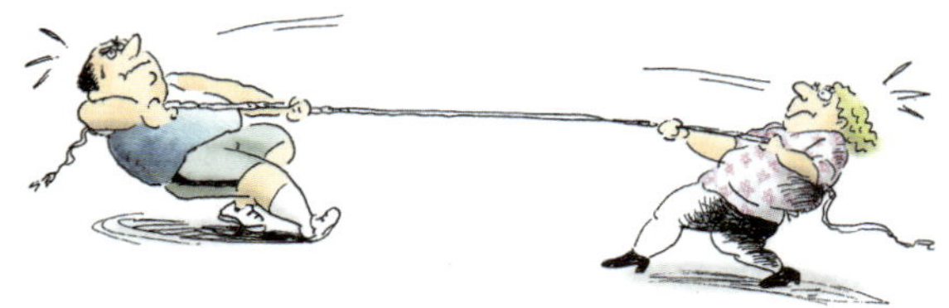

Q1) Who tries to lose weight more often, men or women? Why?

Q2) Which gender is more successful at weight control? Why?

7

Q1) Describe the kinds of diets you have tried.

Q2) Were any of them successful? For how long?

Q1) If you could take a pill that would let you live up to 100 years, would you take it? What if it had terrible side-effects?

Q2) What about a 200-year pill?

# Express Yourself Directly

1. Some people are healthy while others are not. Why?
2. Do you have your own recipe for staying fit?
3. Some doctors say everything about health hinges on individual genes. Do you think so?
4. Fat people are said to be discriminated against when they try to get a job. Do you agree?
5. What's the difference between work and a workout?

— I'm being unfairly discriminated against, just because I don't meet society's artificial standards of beauty.

— You don't meet the qualifications. We're looking for a super model to advertise wedding gowns.

— And you won't hire me because I'm not abnormally skinny.

— No, we're not hiring you because you're not a female.

# Let's Talk Funny

## The Best Time to Work Out

**Woman**: You should exercise more. You're getting fat.

**Man**: I'm thinking about it, but I have a PROBLEM.

**Woman**: What is it?

**Man**: Scientific research says it's not good to exercise in the morning.

**Woman**: Then why don't you do it in the evening?

**Man**: I don't feel good if I exercise after supper.

**Woman**: What about late at night?

**Man**: I'm afraid I won't sleep well.

## Questions

(1) How does the man excuse himself for not exercising?

(2) How can we persuade this kind of person to exercise?

# What Does It Mean?

1

"Happiness is nothing more than good health and bad memory."

2

"Time and health are two precious assets that we don't recognize and appreciate until they have been depleted."

3

Anybody who thinks money is everything has never been sick.

4

Money, achievement, fame, and success are important, but they are bought too dearly if acquired at the cost of health.

5

If you drink too often to other people's health, you'll ruin your own.

These expressions are related to the topics in this chapter. It will be good speaking practice to let students explain what these sentences mean in their own words in English.

6

Mental health has become such an issue today that many people go crazy in pursuit of it.

7

The physical condition of a man can best be judged from what he takes two of at a time — stairs or pills.

8

A health nut has specified in his will that he wishes to be buried in a "no smoking" section of the cemetery.

9

When it comes to eating right and exercising, there is no "I'll start tomorrow." Tomorrow is disease.

10

Medical doctors measure physical health by how the tongue looks. The Great Physician measures spiritual health by how the tongue acts.

1

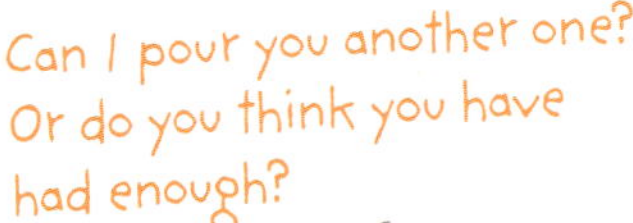

2

10

Think of these cartoons as scenes in a movie. The dialog has been scripted. Now we need actors to play the parts.

9

8

3

And my wife said I don't need to worry, that my cold isn't so bad. But now, in addition to health insurance, I'm afraid I'll need damage insurance too.

4

He used to sing me to sleep, like a baby. Those nights are long gone.

S·y·n·o·p·s·i·s

These are the pictures you've seen in this chapter. It will be good speaking practice for you to talk about these pictures once again. Your teacher will ask you "What are they doing?" or "What does this picture mean?" or some other question. You can give a straight answer or you can use your imagination. The purpose is to allow free conversation; there is no "right" answer.

S·y·n·o·p·s·i·s

5

I run a marathon every week. I take multi-vitamins and supplements every day. I eat healthy meals and don't smoke or drink. And I get plenty of sleep. Why is life so boring?

7

My dieting secret is to eat whatever I like, and smoking helps keep my weight down.

I don't want to smoke, so I limit my diet. Instead of eating from five food groups, I limit myself to two: pizza and wine.

6

— I can lose more weight than you can, any time!
— I could lose 300 pounds of ugly fat in just one day.
— How could you possibly do that?
— By divorcing you.

11

I can't remember ever feeling this great before!

Just thinking about my past depresses me. No wonder I never work out.

12

That alarm clock is too noisy! I'd turn it off if I hadn't broken my leg.

You can shut me down, but you can't turn back time. You should have taken better care of yourself while you still had time.

20

I could say plenty, but I'll let him do all the talking.

Think of these cartoons as scenes in a movie. The dialog has been scripted. Now we need actors to play the parts.

19

Today I want you to start eating regular meals and walking 15 minutes every day.

I don't know, Doc. I don't feel very well. Can I start later when I feel better?

18

I don't understand what the phrase "To Burn in Hell" means if there's no smoking.

13

14

S·Y·N·O·P·S·I·S

These are the pictures you've seen in this chapter. It will be good speaking practice for you to talk about these pictures once again. Your teacher will ask you "What are they doing?" or "What does this picture mean?" or some other question. You can give a straight answer or you can use your imagination. The purpose is to allow free conversation; there is no "right" answer.

S·Y·N·O·P·S·I·S

S·Y·N·O·P·S·I·S

15

By the time they finish their toasts, their own health will be toast.

16

I don't understand how I ever got the nickname "Hamster."

17

I thought following a 12-step program was the key to success, but now I'm falling behind.

# Issue 05 Recreational Activities

## Pictures Talk

1

Q1) List as many indoor and outdoor recreational activities as you can.

Q2) Which ones are expensive and which ones aren't?

2

Q1) Talk about the various kinds of movies and how often you see them.

Q2) Do you usually watch movies at home or in a movie theater? What was the most impressive movie you've ever seen?

3

Q1) What are your favorite sports?

Q2) Do you like to see sports on TV or do you prefer to play them yourself? Why?

4

Q1) What kinds of music do you like? Who's your favorite singer?

Q2) Do you like to sing? Can you play any musical instrument?

Most people need some diversity in their lives. After a while, they grow bored doing the same thing day in and day out, especially when it is work-related. So they want to adopt different routines, see different sights, and test different lifestyles, even if only temporarily. That is why they develop hobbies and take vacations, to vary their mundane existence.

5

Q1) What are some popular video games you're familiar with? What is your favorite?

Q2) Video games are said to be addictive and may damage people's mental health. Do you agree? How can we protect ourselves from becoming a game nut?

6

Q1) Do you like to travel? Where have you gone? Do you have any anecdotes about a trip you would like to share?

Q2) What do you get from traveling around? Do you usually get homesick while you're away?

7

Q1) Some people enjoy extreme sports such as desert marathons or rock climbing, risking their lives. Can you imagine why?

Q2) If your boyfriend or girlfriend did it, would you try to dissuade him or her? Why or why not?

8

Q1) What are the most positive functions of books? What do you personally get from reading?

Q2) How many books do you read a month? Do you mainly read job-related books or books for personal enjoyment?

# Express Yourself Directly

1. Why is recreation important? What does recreation mean to your life?
2. People enjoy fishing and hunting though they are killing living beings. Should we call it a "hobby" or a "barbarous custom"?
3. Do you think gambling should be labeled a "hobby"?
4. Playing golf has become a must for many business people. Why?
5. What's the difference between those who enjoy diverse recreational activities and those who don't?

# Let's Talk Funny

## Vacation Planning Made Simple

**Hubby**: Our vacation time is coming soon!

**Wife**: I'm thinking about where to go and how much we should spend.

**Hubby**: Is there anything I can do to help you?

**Wife**: Of course! Just get some money ready and FOLLOW my plan.

## Questions

(1) Who makes the vacation plans in your family?

(2) Do you feel refreshed or tired after you take a vacation? Why?

# What Does It Mean?

1

A hobby a day keeps the doldrums away.

2

If bread is the first necessity of life, recreation is a close second.

3

I did nothing but work. I made work my hobby. I was lucky that way.

4

Making money is a hobby that will complement any other hobbies you have, beautifully.

5

Missing you is my hobby, caring for you is my job, making you happy is my duty, and loving you is my life.

These expressions are related to the topics in this chapter. It will be good speaking practice to let students explain what these sentences mean in their own words in English.

6

When I die, bury me on the golf course so my husband will visit.

7

We ask this simple question:
Does fishing make people into liars?
Or do only liars fish?

8

People who cannot find time for recreation are obliged sooner or later to find time for illness.

9

The busier we are, the more leisure we have.

10

My biggest worry after I die is that my wife will sell my golf clubs for what I said I paid for them.

1

Motorcycling is my favorite sport because of the speed and excitement, and it's outdoors.

How can you call that a sport? You just sit there on your bike but you don't actually do anything!

2

In scene one, the hero is born. In scene two, he marries his childhood sweetheart. In scene three, he reads her diary and discovers she loves someone else. So, in scene four, one of them has to die. But the victim depends on whether the movie is a comedy or a tragedy.

10

I'll hide my ball before Dad burns it.

**Think of these cartoons as scenes in a movie. The dialog has been scripted. Now we need actors to play the parts.**

9

Watch me make this putt! I'm another Tiger Woods!

Very good. But it took you ten strokes to get your ball on the green.

8

A toothbrush keeps the teeth from decaying, but a book prevents the brain from decaying.

3

Someday I'm going to be the greatest fat footballer in history.

4

The only musical instrument I play well is the iPod.

# S·Y·N·O·P·S·I·S

These are the pictures you've seen in this chapter. It will be good speaking practice for you to talk about these pictures once again. Your teacher will ask you "What are they doing?" or "What does this picture mean?" or some other question. You can give a straight answer or you can use your imagination. The purpose is to allow free conversation; there is no "right" answer.

5

Computer games, cigarettes, ramyun. What else could anyone possibly need to be happy?

7

Did you remember to pack the parachutes?

It's a little late to remind me now, don't you think?

6

Wow, look at that pyramid. And the Sphinx! Someday I'd like to see them in person.

Here are the pyramids. But they're not as impressive as they looked on my computer screen. I should have stayed home.

11

I can hit six balls in the air at the same time. But I can't get even one of them to hit the target.

12

Without bread, I can't enjoy my body or my music. So I need all three.

20

Think of these cartoons as scenes in a movie. The dialog has been scripted. Now we need actors to play the parts.

19

If I were less busy, I wouldn't have any time to do anything.

18

I finally got the time to write my novel, and I only have time enough to write my will.

13

I don't understand. This guy has never worked a day in his life. He sits around all day and plays! But he easily takes away my hard-earned cash.

14

It sure does! But I don't care, I'll just go out and make more of it to support my other expensive tastes.

S·y·n·o·p·s·i·s

These are the pictures you've seen in this chapter. It will be good speaking practice for you to talk about these pictures once again. Your teacher will ask you "What are they doing?" or "What does this picture mean?" or some other question. You can give a straight answer or you can use your imagination. The purpose is to allow free conversation; there is no "right" answer.

S·y·n·o·p·s·i·s

S·y·n·o·p·s·i·s

15

– Will you marry me?
– Do I know you?
– You don't have to. It was love at first sight!

16

Quiet, Dear, you'll make me lose my concentration.

17

This is my 20th catch of the day. How are you doing?

I let him catch me. It's the only way I can listen to their entertaining stories.

I only hooked one. But I couldn't get the harpoons out so I threw it back.

# Issue 06 Jobs

## Pictures Talk

1

Q1) What are some good jobs and some bad ones? List at least five of each.

Q2) What criteria distinguish good jobs from bad ones?

2

Q1) What are your priorities when you search for a job?

Q2) Talk about conditions you can give up and ones you can't when looking for a job.

3

Q1) What do you think is the best job in the world? Is there any job that is easy and makes a lot of money?

Q2) What is the worst job? Which one takes a lot of work and doesn't pay well?

4

Q1) Would you rather work for someone else or be your own boss?

Q2) What are the good things, and the bad ones, about being an employee? An employer?

Most of the time, we work because we need money to live on; almost nobody works for free. The highest-paying jobs also confer the highest status and the most social exposure. But, clearly, some people work for low pay and would never dream of getting a "better" job, or we would not have any teachers, artists, poets, nurses, cab drivers, or soldiers. Money is not the only motivating factor in how we live our lives.

5

Q1) Do you have an impulse to resign? When?

Q2) People always want to say goodbye to their current job, but they don't go ahead with the urge. Why not?

Q1) Some people change their jobs very often, and others don't. What's the difference between these two kinds of people?

Q2) What five things should the jobless do to get a good job?

Q1) Do you think "full-time housekeeper" should be regarded as a real job? Why or why not?

Q2) How much do you think a housekeeper is worth in financial terms?

Q1) Would you consider early retirement if you had enough money to last for the rest of your life? Why or why not?

Q2) Do you have a retirement plan? What is it?

# Express Yourself Directly

1. What do you think about the following jobs? Talk about their merits and demerits.
   (a) farmer
   (b) teacher
   (c) politician
   (d) comedian
   (e) cab driver
   (f) chef
   (g) doctor
   (h) street vendor
   (i) soldier
   (j) househusband
2. Do you think having a job is a must? Why or why not?
3. Is there any way a person can live without a job? If so, how?
4. Do you believe every job is valuable? Why or why not?
5. Who do you think should make more money — blue-color workers or white-color workers? Why?

# Let's Talk Funny

## Life-long Employment

**Woman**: What do you do for a living?

**Man**: I'm a businessman.

**Woman**: What business are you in?

**Man**: Oh, it's always a very promising enterprise, and very lucrative if you have some nerve and determination. It's even tax-free.

**Woman**: What in the world do you do?

**Man**: I'm a PANHANDLER

## Questions

(1) If one of your friends or family members were a panhandler, would you accept him for what he is, or would you be ashamed of him? Why?

(2) What do you think about imposing taxes on panhandlers? Would it be cruel or just?

# What Does It Mean?

1

The best way to appreciate your job is to imagine yourself without one.

2

It's a recession when your neighbor loses his job; it's a depression when you lose yours.

3

I don't care if I were digging ditches at a dollar a day, I'd want to do my job better than the fellow next to me. I'd want to be the best at whatever I do.

4

Being a housewife and mother is the biggest job in the world, but if that doesn't interest you, don't do it — you would make a terrible mom if your heart wasn't in it.

5

Choose a job you love and you will never have to work a day in your life.

These expressions are related to the topics in this chapter. It will be good speaking practice to let students explain what these sentences mean in their own words in English.

6

A baseball game is twice as much fun if you're seeing it on the company's time.

7

When people go to work, they shouldn't have to leave their hearts at home.

8

If you want to be comfortable, take an easy job. If you want to be a leader, take off your coat and roll up your sleeves.

9

It seems a lot of young people want to find an occupation that won't keep them occupied.

10

Don't blame Wall Street, don't blame the big banks. If you don't have a job or you are not rich, blame yourself!

1

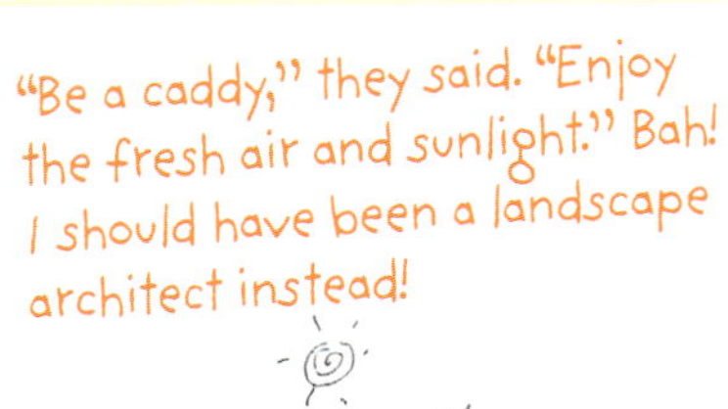

2

What can I do to make the most money?

10

Think of these cartoons as scenes in a movie. The dialog has been scripted. Now we need actors to play the parts.

9

How much can I cut the salaries of my workforce without jeopardizing my own situation?

How many workers does it take to pay for a CEO's membership in a single country club?

8

**3**

Life's not fair! We work diligently every day to make honey, but that lazy guy will take it from us after he finishes his nap.

I guess pretty soon it'll be time to get to "work." Meanwhile, I'll dream about how delicious that honey will taste.

**4**

Should I hire someone else to figure out how to make my job easier? Let me "think" about it.........

I need this job. So I'd better work harder to keep from being fired.

I wish I could afford to stay home and be with the kids. I miss them.

Maybe this time, if I really impress my boss, I can finally get a raise.

## S·Y·N·O·P·S·I·S

These are the pictures you've seen in this chapter. It will be good speaking practice for you to talk about these pictures once again. Your teacher will ask you "What are they doing?" or "What does this picture mean?" or some other question. You can give a straight answer or you can use your imagination. The purpose is to allow free conversation; there is no "right" answer.

S·Y·N·O·P·S·I·S

**5**

Why do I keep you on the payroll? You're the worst employee I've ever had. You should pay ME to work here!

I hate my job and I hate my boss. But I'd hate to be unemployed even more. Maybe I can stick it out a little longer.

**7**

Do I ever get sick leave? Do I get a pension? Do I get vacation time? A bonus? A promotion? Flex-hours? Union representation? Merit pay? Stock options? Workman's compensation?

Stop whining and take care of me!

I'm glad she cleaned this spot for me. I hate pooping on a dirty floor.

**6**

I build my web carefully and well, and I don't want to move it very often. To succeed I need skill and patience.

I've spent my whole life hopping around from place to place, looking for a little happiness, and new opportunities. But I guess last time I should have stayed put!

12

20

I know. I had a nine-figure job, arranging liquidations, downsizings, mergers, and outsourcing. But then there was a hostile takeover, and the next thing I knew I was out of a job.

wall st.

I was in charge of structuring a huge deal involving high-yield derivatives and growth funds. But then the big crash destroyed investor confidence, and it all came tumbling down.

Think of these cartoons as scenes in a movie. The dialog has been scripted. Now we need actors to play the parts.

19

18

I love my job. I get paid for assembling these model homes all day. Who ever thought up these designs anyway?

Trying to figure out how to design these models so any idiot can put them together is hard, frustrating work. But I love the challenge!

13

I hear footsteps approaching. I hope it's a nice fat antelope!

I see a big yellow object ahead! I hope it's cheese!

14

Knowing my baby is sleeping next to me gives me a warm, comfortable feeling of satisfaction. I love my life!

This creature is always giving me trouble. I hate this life!

## S·Y·N·O·P·S·I·S

These are the pictures you've seen in this chapter. It will be good speaking practice for you to talk about these pictures once again. Your teacher will ask you "What are they doing?" or "What does this picture mean?" or some other question. You can give a straight answer or you can use your imagination. The purpose is to allow free conversation; there is no "right" answer.

S·Y·N·O·P·S·I·S

15

I don't know why my wife complains about cooking. I love it!

Who ever thought someone could get paid to run? I love this job!

16

Go, team! Beat those other guys! Destroy them! (I love going to a baseball game when my boss thinks I'm seeing clients)

What's he doing here? It's okay for me to see a game on company time, but HE's supposed to be seeing a client!

17

People complain about how heartless big corporations are, but we should never forget where our hearts are.

We don't just work to make money but also to provide for our family and to contribute to society.

# Issue 07 Time

## Pictures Talk

1

Q1) When is the best time every day?

Q2) When do you think you waste time?

2

Q1) Discuss how you spend a typical 24-hour day.

Q2) What do you do to save time? Do you have any tips you want to share?

3

Q1) Do you think sleeping is a waste of time? Why or why not? What about watching TV? Reading a novel?

Q2) Some adult males say having to spend time in the military is just killing time. Do you agree? Why or why not?

4

Q1) What do you do when you're with your family? Do you enjoy being with other people?

Q2) What do you do when you're alone? Do you ever enjoy being alone?

"Do you have the time?" People say that when they want to know what time it is. But the deeper, implied, questions are, "Do you have the time to do what you want? Do you have enough time to be happy? Or, don't you have time enough? And, if not, why not?" Once our time has come, once its expiration date has arrived, we have no options left, and we cease to exist. But while we have time, we can and should use it to our advantage; "not enough time" is never a valid excuse.

**5**

Q1) Are you an early bird or a night owl?

Q2) Which group, early birds or night owls, spends time more effectively? Why?

**6**

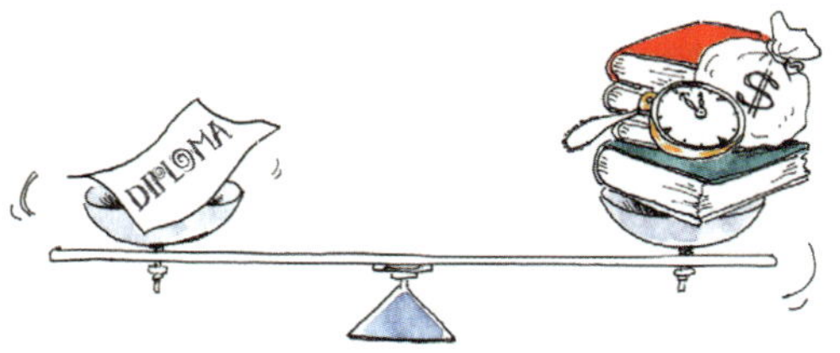


Q1) Is a college education worth the time people invest in it? Why or why not?

Q2) What about the tuition cost? Is the diploma actually worth the price?

**7**

Q1) When do men think women are just wasting their time?

Q2) When do women think men are just wasting their time?

**8**

Q1) Would you be satisfied with a relatively small salary and eight-hour work days, or would you rather work additional hours and make more money? Why?

Q2) Would you consider early retirement to give yourself more time to do what you wish? Why or why not? How would you spend your retirement time?

# Express Yourself Directly

1. If time is money, how much is one hour worth, do you think?
2. Which is better, saving time or saving money?
3. When do you feel time is going too fast? When does time seem to drag?
4. How do you spend your time when you're in a bus, taxi, or subway?
5. As they get older, how do people define time differently than when they were young?

## The Time Is the Same

**Man**: What's the difference between the rich and the poor?

**Friend**: OVERNIGHT

**Man**: What do you mean?

**Friend**: Poor people who win the lottery can get rich overnight, but the rich can lose their fortunes overnight too.

## Questions

(1) Talk about ways to get rich overnight.

(2) Some people say money begets money, so the wealthy can't actually lose their fortunes overnight. Do you agree?

# What Does It Mean?

1

Yesterday is a canceled check; tomorrow is a promissory note; today is the only cash you have — so spend it wisely.

2

Time is the justice that examines all offenders.

3

The time you enjoy wasting time is not wasted time.

4

The time I kill is killing me.

5

If you want work well done, find a busy man to do it — the other kind has no time.

These expressions are related to the topics in this chapter. It will be good speaking practice to let students explain what these sentences mean in their own words in English.

6

Time heals what reason cannot.

7

Time separates the best of friends, and so does money — and marriage!

8

If we take care of the moments, the years will take care of themselves.

9

Too many of us spend our time the way politicians spend our money.

10

If you think time heals everything, try sitting in a doctor's office.

**1**

I love this show! It always provides me an opportunity to nap.

**2**

I'm frazzled every day. There's too much to do and not enough time to do it.

I look forward to the next day, knowing that I will be fresh, alert, happy, and married to a workaholic.

**10**

If I can score a quick knockout, I'll win the fight and make a fortune. But he's bigger than I am, so it's a lot like winning the lottery.

I need to nail this runt right away. The longer the fight lasts, the better his odds become.

## Think of these cartoons as scenes in a movie. The dialog has been scripted. Now we need actors to play the parts.

**9**

Because of this new technology, I can get a lot done very quickly without much work.

Due to this old worn-out technology, everything takes a lot of time and effort to accomplish.

**8**

Time can be your friend — or your enemy! Tick! Tick!

I miss spending time with my friends and family. I never get to spend any time on my hobbies. But if I work very hard now, while I can, I hope to have a very comfortable lifestyle and eventually a nice retirement. But by then my kids will have grown up without me, and my health may be bad. Have I made the wrong choice?

**3**

I love to sleep. I never have to worry or think.

I'm compelled to write this novel, and I can't sleep until I do. But it would be easier to concentrate if I didn't have to listen to his snoring all the time.

**4**

Sometimes I just want to be by myself so I can get my thoughts together and reestablish connection with my inner self. And when my wife has chores for me to do.

## S·Y·N·O·P·S·I·S

These are the pictures you've seen in this chapter. It will be good speaking practice for you to talk about these pictures once again. Your teacher will ask you "What are they doing?" or "What does this picture mean?" or some other question. You can give a straight answer or you can use your imagination. The purpose is to allow free conversation; there is no "right" answer.

S·Y·N·O·P·S·I·S

S·Y·N·O·P·S·I·S

**5**

The early bird gets the worm, they say. But the second mouse gets the cheese! And the owl gets the mouse.

**7**

My wife could be at home watching TV with me. Instead, she's out gallivanting around town, wasting time.

I should be at home cooking, but I'd rather spend my time spending hubby's money.

**6**

Maybe I don't look like much. I'm certainly very thin. But every gram is worth its weight in diamonds.

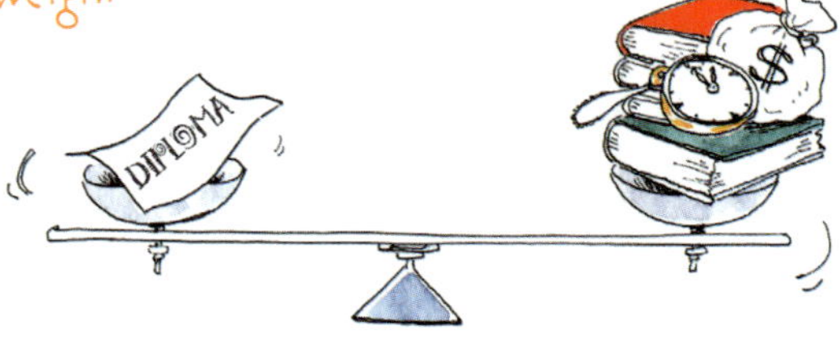


Time is money. Why waste it on a degree when you can use it to get a head start on experience?

11

My past is a disaster, and I don't know what the future looks like. But right now I'm doing the best I can with what I have.

12

As for me, I'm running away from time. It's my only hope.

20

I'm here because I have painful hemorrhoids — and you want me to sit and wait in the doctor's office?

Think of these cartoons as scenes in a movie. The dialog has been scripted. Now we need actors to play the parts.

19

I'm in a hurry to get where I'm going, but I don't mind spending a fortune to get there.

It takes me longer to get where I want, but at least I'll have the resources to enjoy my time there.

18

I ran as hard as I could for as long as I could, never letting up and never giving up.

So, now, I can afford to take it easy and enjoy myself.

**13**

— I could be in the office working on a special project, but then I would have missed out on a great party.
— I'm sure you can work extra hard on it tomorrow.
— I know I can. Especially because this party has reenergized my attitude.
— Would you care for another drink?

**14**

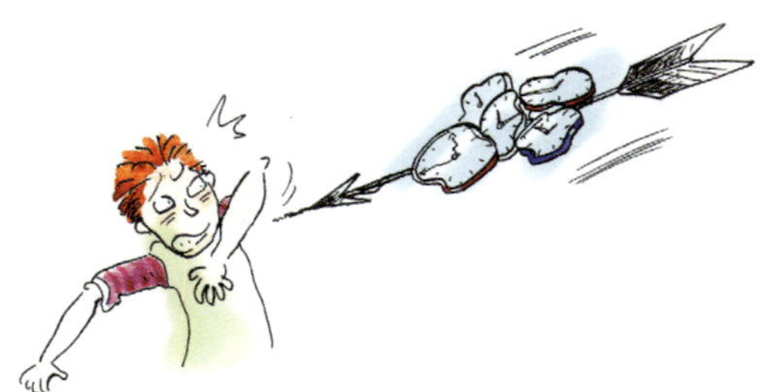

I thought I could make up for lost time, but I didn't know about its multiplier effects.

## S·y·n·o·p·s·i·s

These are the pictures you've seen in this chapter. It will be good speaking practice for you to talk about these pictures once again. Your teacher will ask you "What are they doing?" or "What does this picture mean?" or some other question. You can give a straight answer or you can use your imagination. The purpose is to allow free conversation; there is no "right" answer.

S·y·n·o·p·s·i·s

S·y·n·o·p·s·i·s

**15**

Having so much to do forces me to be efficient. If I didn't have so much to do, I could afford to be pleasantly unproductive.

**17**

You go your way. I'll go mine. But the mountain of life is falling down on me.

I'm sure I'll have my own avalanche on a different mountain.

**16**

Since time cures all wounds, I insert a clock in all my patients.

I hope it's not an alarm clock.

# Issue 08 New You

## Pictures Talk

1

Q1) List some common New Year's resolutions made by ordinary people and discuss your answers.

Q2) Some say, "I won't make any more New Year's resolutions since I always fall short of achieving them." Do you agree with that sentiment? Why or why not?

2

Q1) People say some idling time is needed to charge one's batteries. Is that a correct assessment or just an excuse for being lazy?

Q2) Some say being alone at times is necessary to renew oneself. Discuss this point.

3

Q1) Reading is important in order to change yourself. Do you agree? Why or why not?

Q2) What kinds of books are you interested in? How much time do you devote to them?

4

Q1) What subject do you want to learn about? Why?

Q2) Do you have any particular skills you want to get or improve? What are they?

Knowing you want a change is the easy bit. But knowing where to start can be hard. So plan carefully, take it one step at a time, and you'll be amazed at what you can achieve. Otherwise, the change you get may not be the kind of change you want.

## 5

Q1) What kind of person do you want to be?

Q2) What do you want to be in ten years? Thirty years?

Q1) In order to move on, maybe we should let bygones be bygones. But do you know how to do that? Is there anything that is absolutely unforgivable?

Q2) In order not to worry about the future, what is the best attitude to adopt?

Q1) What should be the first step in making yourself a better person?

Q2) Why is it sometimes difficult to make that first step?

## 8

Q1) What is your philosophy of life? What do you care about the most? What motivates you?

Q2) Is it easy to lead your life in accordance with that philosophy?

# Express Yourself Directly

1. "I'll do it later or tomorrow" is the worst enemy of self-improvement. Do you know how to cope with that attitude?
2. You should count your blessings instead of mourning the past or worrying about what you don't have. Talk about your current blessings.
3. List the most important things in life. How do you think your list compares with that of most people?
4. Some people suffer from addictions such as smoking, drinking, shopping, and gambling. Do you think they just lack willpower? Are they mentally ill? Or is their behavior due to other causes?
5. If you knew you had only one year to live, how would you spend your time? With whom?

Tomorrow I'll start my exercise regime.
Tomorrow I'll begin to diet.
Tomorrow I'll stop wasting time.
Tomorrow, maybe I will die.
So I might as well enjoy myself today.

## Even the Truth Is Fattening

Fast food companies are often criticized for making people fatter and less healthy. But one company thinks the criticism is unfair, so it is holding a press conference with an attractive model to present its case.

**Reporter**: Do you like hamburgers?

**Model**: Yes, of course.

**Reporter**: How about fried chicken?

**Model** : I like it very much.

**Reporter**: What about pizza?

**Model** : Definitely!

**Reporter**: But you are so thin! How often do you eat any of them?

**Model** : Oh, don't ask me that! I'm only supposed to tell you I LIKE these foods, not if I EAT them.

## Questions

(1) Why do you think the model isn't supposed to answer that kind of question?

(2) How often do you eat fast food? Do you usually allow your kids to eat it?

You claim that you never eat fast food. Then how can you advertise it as a model?

If I ate it I wouldn't be thin enough for them to hire me.

# What Does It Mean?

1

A good exercise for the heart is bending down and helping someone to get up.

2

In any family, measles are less contagious than bad habits.

3

If you break the rules in the game of life, the rules will eventually break you.

4

They can because they think they can.

5

Do not wait to strike till the iron is hot, but make it hot by striking.

These expressions are related to the topics in this chapter. It will be good speaking practice to let students explain what these sentences mean in their own words in English.

6

As long as habit and routine dictate the pattern of living, new dimensions of the soul will not emerge.

7

Men's best successes come after their greatest disappointments.

8

A failure is a person who has blundered but is not able to cash in on the experience.

9

Great spirits have always encountered violent opposition from mediocre minds.

10

Finding a way to live a simple life is today's most complicated job.

1

Every year, New Year's Resolutions are the same as the Old Year's Resolutions.

Sitting here alone is just like being with you.

Is that a compliment or an insult?

10

You claim that you never eat fast food. Then how can you advertise it as a model?

If I ate it I wouldn't be thin enough for them to hire me.

Think of these cartoons as scenes in a movie. The dialog has been scripted. Now we need actors to play the parts.

9

Tomorrow I'll start my exercise regime.
Tomorrow I'll begin to diet.
Tomorrow I'll stop wasting time.
Tomorrow, maybe I will die.
So I might as well enjoy myself today.

8

When life takes a turn for the worse, it's easy for us to get derailed. But we must get back on track or we'll never reach our destination.

3

This book iPod is great. I can select the chapter I want, I can put it on random when I'm bored, and I can repeat or delete. Best of all, I can put the entire library on sleep.

These are the pictures you've seen in this chapter. It will be good speaking practice for you to talk about these pictures once again. Your teacher will ask you "What are they doing?" or "What does this picture mean?" or some other question. You can give a straight answer or you can use your imagination. The purpose is to allow free conversation; there is no "right" answer.

S · Y · N · O · P · S · I · S

5

After you have time to repent you'll realize I'm the best friend you have.

6

7

— Thank you for wheeling me around.

— Think nothing of it. It's good exercise for my heart.

— In both senses of the word "heart."

12

Whether or not I smoke is my own business. It doesn't affect anyone else.

I guess, if he does it, smoking must be good for him. So I'll try it too.

20

When I was young, a hamburger and a soft drink were regarded as a very simple snack. Now burgers come in many styles and sizes, with lots of optional ingredients added; and sodas are in many flavors and quantities. Eating out is not only more complicated but also more expensive.

**Think of these cartoons as scenes in a movie. The dialog has been scripted. Now we need actors to play the parts.**

19

We can't imagine anything greater.

We like our little lives.

So we have to put obstacles in the path of change.

If nobody is bigger, we can't be mediocre.

Let's try something better.

18

The tape at the finish line keeps moving! How can I ever cross it?

13

I thought it would be a blast to break the rules, so I played with dynamite all my life. But now my careless defiance has exploded in my face.

14

People who tried to walk on water have always failed. But they should have tried running instead.

## S·Y·N·O·P·S·I·S

These are the pictures you've seen in this chapter. It will be good speaking practice for you to talk about these pictures once again. Your teacher will ask you "What are they doing?" or "What does this picture mean?" or some other question. You can give a straight answer or you can use your imagination. The purpose is to allow free conversation; there is no "right" answer.

S·Y·N·O·P·S·I·S

15

You hold it tight and I'll keep hitting it.

Isn't it hot yet?

17

I really took a beating, but I guess I finally won.

You knocked your opponent clear out of the ring.

16

Just when I'm ready to get going, I feel weighed down by my habits.

# Why We Shop?

## Pictures Talk

Q1) How often do you go shopping? What do you usually buy?

Q2) Where do you usually go to shop? Why?

Q1) When do you go on a shopping spree?

Q2) Why do we sometimes buy non-essentials?

Q1) Do you always wait until sellers offer some discount? Why or why not?

Q2) If you were buying something at a normal price, would you feel ripped off?

Q1) Do you like to buy on the installment plan? Why or why not?

Q2) There is an old saying, "If people were able to buy something on credit, everybody would buy everything." Explain what it means.

Shopping has been described as the new religion; malls are its cathedrals, and sales are its prayers and liturgies. If shopping is an almost religious experience, who are the ministers? What is its bible? What are its spiritual rewards?

5

Q1) Some say they shop to relieve stress. What's their point? Do you understand that feeling?

Q2) My wife says, "If I didn't go shopping once in a while, I would suffer from depression." Should we believe her, or is it just a lame excuse?

Q1) Is grocery shopping fun or drudgery? Why?

Q2) What is the most enjoyable kind of shopping? Why?

Q1) Should we blame overspending on advertisers? Why or why not?

Q2) Do people really believe that ads or commercials tell the truth?

Q1) Which do you prefer — shopping on-line or off-line?

Q2) Which do you think triggers overspending? Or is there no difference? Why?

# Express Yourself Directly

1. Some shopaholics attribute their behavior to human "Buyology" and claim it is a natural response. Do you side with them? Why or why not?
2. Are makes or brands important to you? Why or why not?
3. What's the difference between men and women in the ways they shop?
4. When you return something you bought, do you feel sorry or do you merely regard it as a consumer's right? Are there any reasons for returning it that are really unjustifiable?
5. When it comes to credit-card debt, who is more responsible — consumers, card companies, or the government?

# Let's Talk Funny

## Making Those Special Days Memorable

**Man:** My wife complained that I always forgot to get her something for her birthday. So she took my credit card and said she would get her own presents.

**Friend:** That's good. Now you don't have to worry about remembering her birthday.

**Man:** I don't have to remember it anymore, but I CAN'T FORGET IT.

**Friend:** Why not?

**Man:** It's always the day when she buys herself the most expensive gifts.

## Questions

(1) What would happen if you forgot your sweetheart's birthday?

(2) How do you celebrate your sweetheart's birthday? How do you celebrate your own?

# What Does It Mean?

1

The quickest way to know a woman is to go shopping with her.

2

Whoever said money can't buy happiness simply didn't know where to go shopping.

3

I always say shopping is cheaper than going to a psychiatrist.

4

I haven't reported my missing credit card to the police, because whoever stole it is spending less than my wife.

5

I have been shopping all my life and still have nothing to wear.

These expressions are related to the topics in this chapter. It will be good speaking practice to let students explain what these sentences mean in their own words in English.

6

A bargain isn't a bargain if it's something you don't need.

7

Those who live within their means suffer from a serious lack of imagination.

8

I don't shop to live,
I just live to shop.

9

Too many people spend money they haven't earned, to buy things they don't want, to impress people they don't like.

10

Buying on credit is much like being drunk. The buzz comes immediately and gives you a lift. The hangover comes the day after and lasts longer.

1

They don't sell garage at a garage sale, and they don't sell yards at a yard sale.

2

I'm going on a shopping spree in Singapore next week. So I need to buy some new clothes for the trip.

10

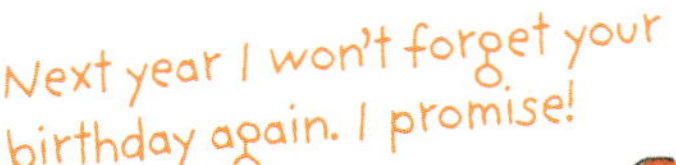

I hope you do. Then you can let me have your credit card again.

## Think of these cartoons as scenes in a movie. The dialog has been scripted. Now we need actors to play the parts.

9

Yes, I'm glad my husband was finally able to take a vacation with me. We're having a marvelous time.

I thought I was taking a holiday in order to relax. I don't have to work this hard when I'm on the job.

8

On-line shopping is wonderful. I never realized I could spend so much money so quickly — and in my living room. So when I go broke, at least I don't have to go far.

3

Wow! 50% off! Maybe I should wait until it's 90%.

4

I saw the sign and didn't realize that it meant the daily installment payment for three years.

## S·Y·N·O·P·S·I·S

These are the pictures you've seen in this chapter. It will be good speaking practice for you to talk about these pictures once again. Your teacher will ask you "What are they doing?" or "What does this picture mean?" or some other question. You can give a straight answer or you can use your imagination. The purpose is to allow free conversation; there is no "right" answer.

S·Y·N·O·P·S·I·S

S·Y·N·O·P·S·I·S

5

It's also true that shopping is the Number One Cause of Depression.

7

Those Twinkies don't say anything, but I still hear them call my name over the airwaves.

6

I want to hurry up and get my grocery shopping done. So I can go to the department store for some jewelry.

11

This is the third store she's gone into, but I haven't seen her buy anything yet. This is the woman I want to marry.

12

I feel so good about shopping here!

That's because everything has the "Happiness" brand name.

20

The headache from a hangover is temporary, but the one from my credit card never ends.

Think of these cartoons as scenes in a movie. The dialog has been scripted. Now we need actors to play the parts.

19

It's time to get rid of all the useless things I accumulated over the years, so I can start getting more.

18

I'm running out of space. I need a bigger house.

13

My husband says spending so much on clothes is nuts, but he hasn't seen what the shrink charges.

14

I'm going shopping. Thanks for letting me use your credit card.

That's quite all right, Dear. Enjoy yourself.

Louie, she's leaving the house now. Make sure you grab that credit card before she has a chance to use it.

Don't worry about a thing. I'll have it in no time.

S·Y·N·O·P·S·I·S

These are the pictures you've seen in this chapter. It will be good speaking practice for you to talk about these pictures once again. Your teacher will ask you "What are they doing?" or "What does this picture mean?" or some other question. You can give a straight answer or you can use your imagination. The purpose is to allow free conversation; there is no "right" answer.

S·Y·N·O·P·S·I·S

S·Y·N·O·P·S·I·S

15

Are you opening a clothing boutique in your bedroom?

No. But I need more closet space. We have to move.

17

— I don't like French fries. Would you like to have them?
— If you weren't going to eat them, why did you buy them?
— They were a special price, and I can't pass up a bargain.

16

If I hadn't bought this giant screen TV I wouldn't be able to see this commercial for reduced-price giant screen TVs. It's a much better price than my other ones.

# Issue 10 Is Your Pet a Family Member?

## Pictures Talk

1

Q1) What are some reasons people have pets?

Q2) Can you think of any reasons some people don't want pets?

2

Q1) Is your pet a family member or just a toy?

Q2) What are the responsibilities of raising a pet?

3

Q1) Do you walk your dog or cat every day?

Q2) What is the proper etiquette to practice when you go out with your pet?

4

Q1) Some people say if you can't love animals, you can't love humans. Do you agree?

Q2) What do you think about people who adore animals but don't pay any attention to needy humans?

ets are not just animals, like livestock. They are an integral part of the family. They are given names and ted like human beings (often better than human beings). They are pampered, primped, and lavished with e and affection. If they are sick, they are taken care of; when dead, buried with honor and devotion. They are talked to and regularly consulted. Most spouses would like to get the same loving care their pets receive!

5

Q1) If your pet could talk, what do you think they would most often tell you?

Q2) Can you read your pet's mind? Can your pet read your mind?

6

Q1) What do you think of pet owners who say, "My dog is too well-behaved to be kept on a leash"?

Q2) Some people try to bring their pets into public places such as supermarkets or even restaurants. They insist their pets are hygienic. What do you think?

7

Q1) What do you think about lost or abandoned pets? Why are there so many?

Q2) Have you ever taken any of them home?

8

Q1) Do you know what happens to stray animals?

Q2) What should the government do about strays? Take care of them for the rest of their lives? Find homes for them? Ignore them?

# Express Yourself Directly

1. What's the difference between pet people and non-pet people?
2. If your pet were sick and needed an expensive operation, would you pay for it? Or would it be time to consider euthanasia?
3. Suppose you are in a sinking boat with a stranger and your dog and you have only two life jackets. Would you give up your dog to save a fellow human's life?
4. If government introduced a pet-tax, would you support it?
5. What do you think about raising pets in an apartment?

# Let's Talk Funny

## Pet Peeves

**Wife**: I want to have a pet dog.

**Husband**: Okay, but on one condition.

**Wife**: What is it?

**Husband**: Promise me you will treat me as well as you treat the dog.

**Wife**: Sure, but I have a condition too.

**Husband**: What's that?

**Wife**: You should clean up after the dog just like I have to clean up after you.

## Questions

(1) Do you think you are paid as much attention in your family as your pet is?

(2) Who takes care of your pet at home? What is the pet's ranking at home?

# What Does It Mean?

1

Pets are such agreeable friends — they ask no questions, they make no criticisms.

2

A dog is the only thing on earth that will love you more than you love yourself.

3

Don't accept your dog's admiration as conclusive evidence that you are wonderful.

4

A house is not a home without a pet.

5

A dog has so many friends because he wags his tail, not his tongue.

6

To insult someone we call him "bestial." For deliberate cruelty and nature, "human" might be the greater insult.

7

Women and cats will do as they please, and men and dogs should relax and get used to the idea.

8

If people were superior to animals, they'd take better care of the world.

9

If you pick up a starving dog and make him prosperous, he will not bite you. This is the principal difference between a dog and a man.

10

On the Internet, nobody knows you're a dog.

1

2

10

Think of these cartoons as scenes in a movie. The dialog has been scripted. Now we need actors to play the parts.

9

8

3

When my wife wanted to buy a dog, she insisted it would be easy to care for.

What're you complaining about? I thought I was just supposed to wag my tail and be cute, and I'd get a free meal.

4

Don't pay any attention to that dirty creature on the street.

Whoever said "it's a dog's life" didn't know what he was talking about.

Humph!

These are the pictures you've seen in this chapter. It will be good speaking practice for you to talk about these pictures once again. Your teacher will ask you "What are they doing?" or "What does this picture mean?" or some other question. You can give a straight answer or you can use your imagination. The purpose is to allow free conversation; there is no "right" answer.

S · y · n · o · p · s · i · s

5

Dear Tom: I just want to thank you for all the loving care and to complain about the selfish, nasty character of the cat. Can't you get rid of him? He serves no useful purpose.

Hey, Tom! Aren't you concerned about — or even aware of — your dog's bad manners? His constant barking gets on my nerves, and he's always digging up the nice-looking yard. Either he goes, or I do!

6

But these are not pets! They're my guests! They're certainly better behaved than most of the people who eat here.

I feel like a victim of species discrimination.

The food probably isn't very good anyway.

I wasn't really hungry. Let's go home and cook in.

7

I can understand how someone might lose a dog or a cat — they're so many of them. But, a pig?

I'm hungry.

I'm sure I can find my owner somewhere, if I keep looking.

Don't they love me anymore? Don't they miss me?

I hope my owners are all right. I'm worried about them.

11

12

20

I'm considered to be quite tall, but I don't think I would ever qualify for the NBA.

I hate to brag, but most of my friends consider me to be very handsome.

Why can't people be honest on these dating sites? Sooner or later, they'll be uncovered as the liars they are.

Yes, I graduated with an MBA last year. What about you?

The biggest problem is: How can I be sure the person I'm talking to is being truthful?

**Think of these cartoons as scenes in a movie. The dialog has been scripted. Now we need actors to play the parts.**

19

Stop it! What would you be without me?

Happy!

18

**13**

Nice to meet you. I hope you meet with Jock's approval. His judgment is very important to me.

Yes, I agree. That's why I brought Candy along. She's such a marvelous judge of character.

Hi, Candy, I don't care about her, but you're very sweet.

Oh, my. I don't think this couple will work out. They just don't match.

Thank you, Jock. You're pretty terrific too

Which couple? The one with two legs or four?

**14**

I'm glad HE moved out. It was getting too crowded in here.

It's nice to have a place where I can relax and read in peace.

S·Y·N·O·P·S·I·S

These are the pictures you've seen in this chapter. It will be good speaking practice for you to talk about these pictures once again. Your teacher will ask you "What are they doing?" or "What does this picture mean?" or some other question. You can give a straight answer or you can use your imagination. The purpose is to allow free conversation; there is no "right" answer.

S·Y·N·O·P·S·I·S

**15**

Help! That man is dangerous!

Hurry up before he gets you.

I hope he isn't rabid.

I'm going as fast as my little legs can carry me.

**16**

No dog would ever act like those people.

What's the matter with her? We didn't do anything.

I guess loving a dog is better than loving only oneself.

Certainly not any of my friends.

All you did was say that some people love their pets more than they love other people.

**17**

That shade looks good on you, Miss Kitty.

Ah, women! It takes them forever to get ready to go out.

Why can't they be like us? We never need any special preparation. We're always fine as we are.

Thank you. It shows off my whiskers nicely, don't you think?

# Issue 11 One Man's Garbage Is Another Man's Treasure

## Pictures Talk

1

Q1) I think my family should be willing to help me under any circumstances, financially or emotionally. Am I right?

Q2) My parents think even adult kids need discipline. Are they right?

2

Q1) My husband thinks he should be the boss because he's the breadwinner. Is he right?

Q2) I'm a full-time stay-at-home mom. If my husband thinks he's the boss, I'll just quit work. Then he'll change his tune! Do you agree?

3

Q1) The poor think the rich should help them. Are they right?

Q2) The rich think they don't have to help the poor because helping them only makes them stay poor. What do you think?

4

Q1) Some people think taxes on the rich should be raised dramatically to balance the budget. Do you agree?

Q2) The rich insist that high taxes on them diminish their investment ability so it actually kills job opportunities for average people. What's your take?

We all have views about many things, which we have gained from our particular experiences. We wonder why others have such radically different opinions, without stopping to think that no one else has lived life the way we have. Not even identical twins have had precisely the same existence. So it is no wonder there are so many different perspectives on similar issues. But the first step toward wisdom, and the first step toward worldly success as well, is to develop the ability to understand how others feel and why they feel that way.

5

Q1) People have elected me president. They should follow my lead. Am I right?

Q2) Some think their president is only an errand boy, and the people are the masters. Are they right?

6

Q1) Employers think workers should always do their best on the job. Are they right?

Q2) Employees think their work should reflect their salary and benefits. Is it a good attitude? Why or why not?

7

Q1) Criminals think society is responsible for their bad behavior. Does that make sense?

Q2) Some people think the rising crime rate is due to overly-permissive laws. They say, "If laws were stricter, there would be fewer crimes." Do you think so?

8

Q1) The government says it can't lower the price of gas because doing so encourages over-consumption. It that true?

Q2) Drivers say cars are necessary for modern life, so gas prices must be affordable. Are they right?

# Express Yourself Directly

1. Drivers think pedestrians ignore traffic rules, and pedestrians blame drivers. Talk about the viewpoint of each group.
2. Patients think there are too many unqualified doctors, but doctors think patients want to diagnose themselves. Who are right?
3. Elderly people think youngsters lack experience; young people think the old are out of touch. Can they both be right? Explain your answer in detail.
4. Women think men never mature, and men think women grow up too soon and lose their sense of fun. What do you think?
5. You think everybody is wrong while everybody else thinks you are. Is this always the case?
6. Some people say the purpose may justify a bad method, but others think ends never justify means. Which side do you take?

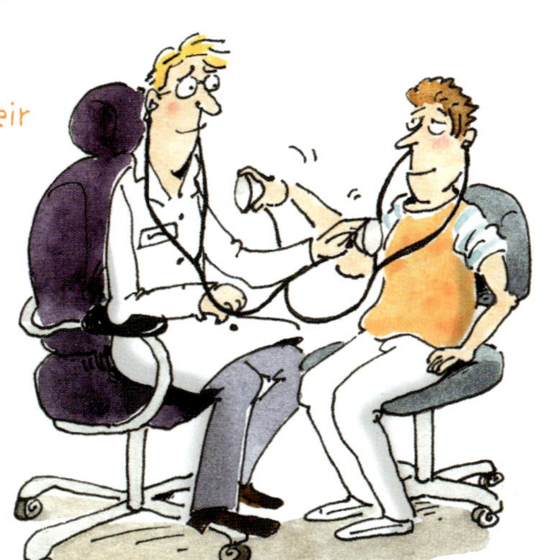

## Divinity According to Species

**Dog**: Those humans offer me food, love, and shelter. So I worship them. They must be my gods.

**Cat**: That's interesting. I think I must be their god, because they offer me food, love, and shelter.

**Dog**: Why do we look at the same situation so differently?

**Cat**: I'm a cat and you're a dog.

**Dog**: What do you mean?

**Cat**: I'm superior to you.

**Dog**: How come?

**Cat**: Don't you know C comes before D?

## Questions

(1) With which pet do you most agree?

(2) Which do you prefer as a pet, a dog or a cat? Why?

(3) Talk about how dogs and cats differ.

— Cats are superior to dogs. And to people, too.
— That's NOT true! How many bones can you bury?
— At least cats would remember where they're buried!

# What Does It Mean?

1

Common sense is the collection of prejudices acquired by age eighteen.

2

I know with what weapons World War III will be fought, but World War IV will then be fought with sticks and stones.

3

A lawyer will do anything to win a case; sometimes he will even tell the truth.

4

You can get much further with a kind word and a gun than you can with a kind word alone.

5

If it weren't for electricity we'd all be watching television by candlelight.

These expressions are related to the topics in this chapter. It will be good speaking practice to let students explain what these sentences mean in their own words in English.

6

They called it golf because all the other four-letter words were taken.

7

If you want anything said, ask a man; if you want anything done, ask a woman.

8

I have three pets, so I don't need a husband. My dog growls every morning, my parrot swears all afternoon, and my cat comes home late every night.

9

An acquaintance is someone we know well enough to borrow from but not enough to lend to.

10

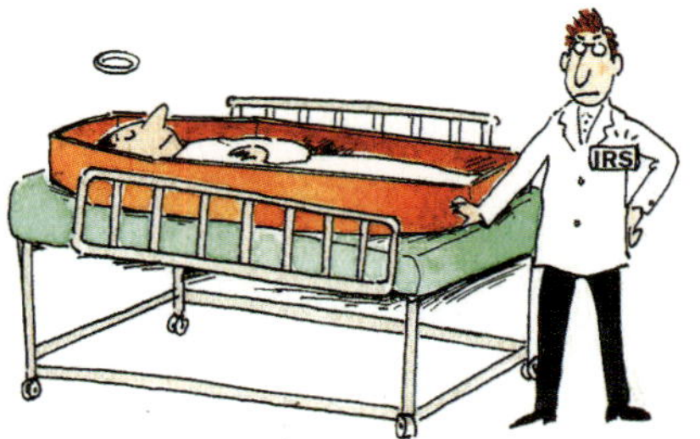


The only difference between death and taxes is that death doesn't get worse every time Congress meets.

1

2

10

Think of these cartoons as scenes in a movie. The dialog has been scripted. Now we need actors to play the parts.

9

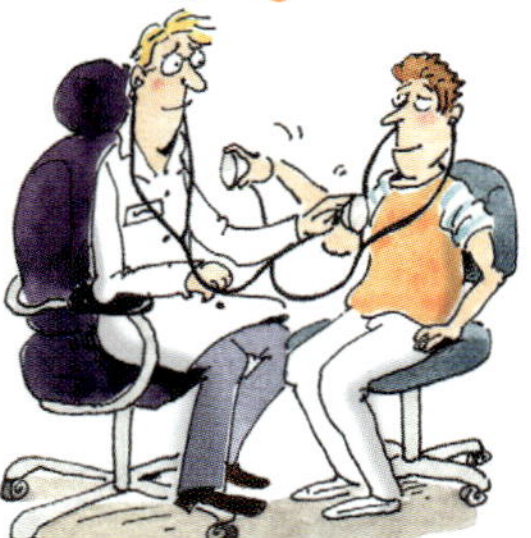


8

3

— Please help me feed my family.
— I have enough difficulty to feed my own. Get a job!
— Panhandling is my job. I earned a degree in it.

4

The wealthiest person can eventually be brought down by a diligent taxman.

# S·Y·N·O·P·S·I·S

These are the pictures you've seen in this chapter. It will be good speaking practice for you to talk about these pictures once again. Your teacher will ask you "What are they doing?" or "What does this picture mean?" or some other question. You can give a straight answer or you can use your imagination. The purpose is to allow free conversation; there is no "right" answer.

S·Y·N·O·P·S·I·S

S·Y·N·O·P·S·I·S

5

You gave me the power to lead. Why won't you follow?

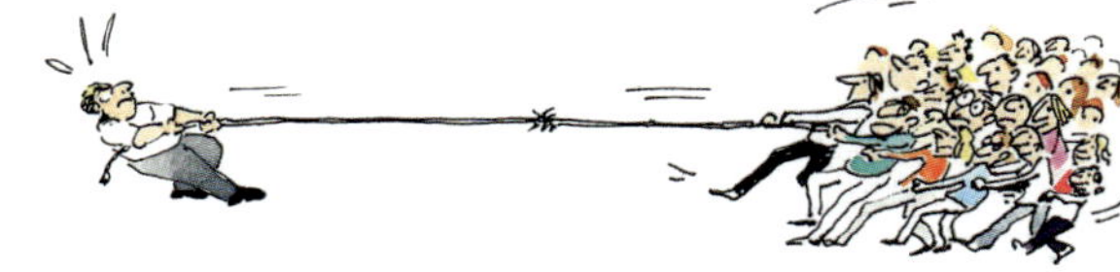

We elected you to follow our will

7

To have a law-abiding citizenry, we need a well-armed police.

Yikes! Let's get out of here before it's too late!

Next time, I'll bring a cannon to defend myself.

Why stop there? We should bring a tank.

6

I hope those ungrateful employees of mine don't think "quitting time" means it's time to go home.

Whew, it's an hour past quitting time, and I'm not finished yet.

I stopped working hours ago. If I ever finish, I'm afraid I won't have a job tomorrow.

11

I insist on acting on my beliefs. Because I know I'm right!

Now that I'm old, I wonder what happened to my former certainties.

12

I demand an end to Neolithic proliferation for the good of humanity.

Put down your weapon first, and then maybe I'll put mine down.

20

I wish I had died BEFORE I paid my taxes. At least then people could say I died a rich man.

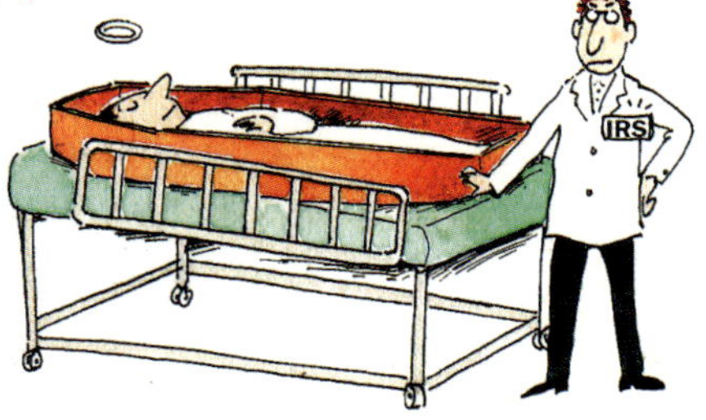


Like they say, "You can't take it with you." But WE can always take it!

Think of these cartoons as scenes in a movie. The dialog has been scripted. Now we need actors to play the parts.

19

My problem is that the friends I have are either broke or know me too well to give me a loan. So I need to make a lot of new friends, real friends who won't expect to get their money back.

18

Please marry me, I love you!

Thanks, but I have many pets. If I married you, it would be mere duplication — or maybe polygamy.

**13**

Remember, students, in a court of law the truth is always your enemy. You must avoid it at all costs, even if it tends to exonerate your client.

I guess if I tell him he is a brilliant lecturer I will be ready to pass the bar exam.

**14**

— You're a very polite mugger.
— Thank you for the kind words.
— That's quite all right. I'm very grateful.
— And I'm grateful, too. Thank you for all your cash.
— So long.
— Good-bye. Maybe we'll meet again.
— I hope so. My treat!

## S·Y·N·O·P·S·I·S

These are the pictures you've seen in this chapter. It will be good speaking practice for you to talk about these pictures once again. Your teacher will ask you "What are they doing?" or "What does this picture mean?" or some other question. You can give a straight answer or you can use your imagination. The purpose is to allow free conversation; there is no "right" answer.

S·Y·N·O·P·S·I·S

S·Y·N·O·P·S·I·S

**15**

I finally get a night off from work, and the electricity goes out. But I'm going to watch TV tonight no matter what. I haven't seen any television shows in years.

Usually when he turns on the TV he goes right to sleep. But now he wants to stay up for a blank screen?

**17**

Who said a woman can't do a man's job? But, very few men can successfully do "woman's work."

**16**

It's a short putt. People are waiting. Why don't you hurry up?

This is a very tricky green. It looks like the ground slopes to the right, but actually it tilts leftward. And if I hit the ball too hard I'll overshoot the hole, but I have to make sure to hit it hard enough to get to the hole. But if I can just blow it into the hole, I'll save at least one stroke from my score.

# Issue 12 What's Normal and What's Not?

## Pictures Talk

1

Q1) I won't lend money to my friends. If they don't pay me back, I'll lose both my money and my friend. Am I too sensitive about this?

Q2) If I lent money to my friend, I would charge interest. Isn't that proper?

2

Q1) I buy lottery tickets every week. Am I normal?

Q2) Why do people buy tickets even though they know the odds of winning are so low as to be mathematically impossible?

3

Q1) I don't deposit my money because of today's low interest rate and high inflation. Am I normal?

Q2) What do you think the best investment, the one that brings the handsomest profit, is? Should profitability outfactor morality in the market?

4

Q1) When I have a date, I ask my partner to go Dutch. Am I normal?

Q2) When you have a date, how do you divvy up the expense?

In the West, people in mourning wear black, while in the East they wear white. In some societies, having several wives is a mark of distinction; in others, it is a criminal offense. We are all human, with the same inherent sense of normal and odd, but our circumstances and expectations vary so widely that it is impossible to define those terms universally.

5

Q1) I'm in my twenties, young, and healthy. So I don't think I need to exercise. Am I normal?

Q2) When is the best time in life to begin exercising? Never? In the teens? By middle age? Some other time?

Q1) I feel offended when other cars go faster than mine. Am I normal?

Q2) What is your average speed on the highway? How often do you get a speeding ticket?

Q1) I want to live in a metropolis despite the busy traffic, noise, pollution, and expense. Am I normal?

Q2) Talk about why people want to live in a big city.

Q1) If my friend buys the newest thing, I'm dying to buy the same thing, even on credit. Am I normal?

Q2) Do you know any method to resist buying on impulse?

# Express Yourself Directly

1. I want to live more than 100 years. Am I normal?
2. I think getting married is nonsense, considering the high divorce rate and the expense. Am I normal?
3. We all badmouth our boss behind his back. Are we normal?
4. I feel anxious when I'm disconnected from my smart phone. Am I normal?
5. I'm an atheist. Am I normal?
6. I don't think everybody is pure. Am I normal?
7. I believe the rich have made their fortune honestly. Am I normal?

I wish I had a boss to complain about.

# Let's Talk Funny

## Ten Degrees of Disability

(The government has just announced a special tax *break* for the handicapped. Many people have gathered at the proper office in order to register.)

**First man:** I'm short compared to other people. So I'm physically handicapped.

**Second man:** I'm a drunkard. So I'm socially handicapped.

**Third man:** I'm *bankrupt*. So I'm financially handicapped.

**Fourth man:** I have a hot temper. So I'm attitudinally handicapped.

**Fifth man:** I have at least one new *love affair* every six months. So I'm morally handicapped.

**Sixth man:** I'm a *burglar*. So I'm *legally* handicapped.

**Seventh man:** I'm a con artist. So I'm empathetically handicapped.

**Eighth man:** I *believe* Murphy's Law actually operates. So I'm scientifically handicapped.

**Ninth man:** I'm divorced. So I'm maritally handicapped.

**Tenth man:** I'm a habitual procrastinator. So I'm chronologically handicapped.

**Eleventh man:** I'm too ugly, so I'm photogenically handicapped.

(The official, at a *loss* as how to classify all these claims, puts them all in the category of MENTALLY HANDICAPPED.)

## Questions

(1) Do you agree with the official? Why or why not?

(2) Who do you think is the most fatefully handicapped among the eleven?

(3) Who is more *seriously troubled*, one who is physically handicapped or mentally handicapped? Why?

# What Does It Mean?

1

Normal is in the eye of the beholder.

2

All people are normal until you get to know them.

3

Normal people don't just wake up in the morning and say, "I think it'd be a good idea to run for president of the United States."

4

To be normal is the ideal of the unsuccessful.

5

I shouldn't say I'm looking forward to leading a normal life, because I don't know what normal is.

*These expressions are related to the topics in this chapter. It will be good speaking practice to let students explain what these sentences mean in their own words in English.*

**6**

To refuse awards is another way of accepting them with more than the usual noise and attention.

**7**

For me, insanity is hyper-sanity; normal is merely psychotic. "Normal" means lack of imagination, lack of creativity.

**8**

People concern themselves with being normal, rather than natural.

**9**

What is a normal childhood? We weren't rich, we were pretty middle-class. My dad survived from job to job; with him taking care of so many relatives, he couldn't save any money.

**10**

The New York Times

How the iPad Mini compares

As advertising blather becomes the nation's normal idiom, language becomes printed noise.

1

2

The odds against winning the lottery are millions to one, but the odds of getting rich any other way are infinity to one.

10

I worry that the rich will eventually figure out a foolproof way to keep me from stealing their wealth.

I don't have enough money to enjoy the finer things of life — like eating, for example. So, I drink to drown out my sorrows.

I have too much money. I'm afraid I'll lose it all.

Think of these cartoons as scenes in a movie. The dialog has been scripted. Now we need actors to play the parts.

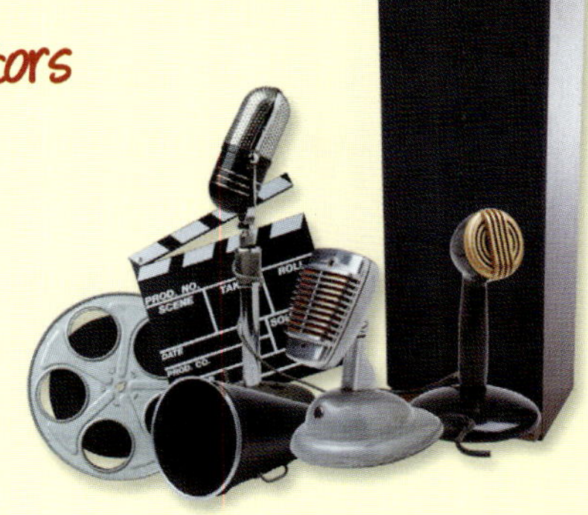

9

The boss cares nothing about his employees.

The boss hasn't given me a raise in five years.

The boss refuses to promote me despite my qualifications.

The boss expects too much free overtime from us.

The boss is a skinflint.

The boss is a sexist.

Mr. BOSS

I wish I had a boss to complain about.

8

If I see the newest fashions, I can't help myself. I have to buy something.

But how do you keep from smelling them?

**3**

ARRRGH! I'll consume everything in my endless quest for profit. I'm already too big to fail, and I continue to grow. ARRRGH!

The bank interests are too big and powerful. We need better regulation.

Don't you believe in free enterprise?

**4**

Thank you for inviting me to dinner. But I misunderstood. I thought you were going to pay for my meal, and so I didn't bring my money.

I'm sorry to hear that. But going Dutch is a matter of principle for me. Maybe I'll have some leftovers I can give you.

# S·Y·N·O·P·S·I·S

These are the pictures you've seen in this chapter. It will be good speaking practice for you to talk about these pictures once again. Your teacher will ask you "What are they doing?" or "What does this picture mean?" or some other question. You can give a straight answer or you can use your imagination. The purpose is to allow free conversation; there is no "right" answer.

S·Y·N·O·P·S·I·S

S·Y·N·O·P·S·I·S

**5**

I should have started exercising when I was younger. Then maybe it wouldn't be so hard.

I have almost figured out how to combine taking exercise with taking a nap. But so far, I still have too much exercise and too little nap.

The half hour of exercise I get every day lets me work and then enjoy myself an extra 2 or 3 hours every day — and will give me many years of extended, healthy life.

**6**

I feel sorry for all those people in slow cars.

I'm tired of folks like you who think you have a right to go faster than I. I'd go faster, if I could.

**7**

I've figured out how combine the simplicity and rigor of country living with the excitement and ease of urban life.

11

I have a lot of female friends, so I decided to dress like them.

I am against sexual discrimination. So everyone should dress the same way.

12

I used to think you were normal, until I got to know you better.

I never thought you were normal, and I still don't.

20

"All the news that's fit to print" — and the editor decides what's proper and profitable for us.

Think of these cartoons as scenes in a movie. The dialog has been scripted. Now we need actors to play the parts.

19

For us, this is normal!

It must be strange for people to stay in one place all the time, to keep the same job, and not to have to worry about getting a flat tire.

18

I still don't run the marathon in the average time. What's wrong with me?

If God had wanted us to be skinny he would have given us liposuction.

I'm happy with the way I am, and the way you are.

13

Normally when I wake up I just want to go back to sleep.

14

I'm looking forward to a normal life.

I wish I had set my sights higher when I was young. Then maybe my life would not have been so mediocre.

## S·Y·N·O·P·S·I·S

These are the pictures you've seen in this chapter. It will be good speaking practice for you to talk about these pictures once again. Your teacher will ask you "What are they doing?" or "What does this picture mean?" or some other question. You can give a straight answer or you can use your imagination. The purpose is to allow free conversation; there is no "right" answer.

S·Y·N·O·P·S·I·S

S·Y·N·O·P·S·I·S

15

If everyone rode a unicycle, I'd fit right in.

No, even if we did we would still think you're odd, because of all of your weird ideas and strange habits.

As for me, I still have trouble riding a bike. I wish I still used my tricycle. That was very easy.

16

We want to present you with the trophies for winning the football game and for being named MVP.

Please don't honor me or gratify my ego!

Please accept this small token of appreciation.

The Nobel Prize Committee would like you to reconsider.

17

Why do people only walk on their feet? They miss out on seeing the world up close and being able to smell reality.

# Issue 13 Is Stress a Foe or a Friend?

## Pictures Talk

1

Q1) Nobody's free from stress. What are some common stresses?

Q2) Is stress always a foe? When can it be a friend?

2

Q1) What are the top five jobs which cause a lot of stress?

Q2) Talk about jobs people can do without stress.

3

Q1) What are the stresses that husbands are likely to suffer from? What are the stresses wives go through?

Q2) Do you think your kids are without stress? What stresses are they usually under?

4

Q1) Who undergoes more stress, a childless couple or one with kids?

Q2) There is an old saying; Half of your life is ruined by your parents and the other half by your kids. Can you explain what it means?

People like to believe that if they had more time and less pressure, they could achieve more and be happier. But these same people seldom use their free time to accomplish anything; they perform only when they are up against a deadline or a threat.

Q1) What are the stresses on most employers? What about employee stress?

Q2) Which group suffers more? Why?

Q1) Does learning English give you a lot of stress? Why or why not?

Q2) What is the solution?

Q1) Different people deal with stress differently. What are some positive ways of dealing with it?

Q2) What happens if someone does not handle stress adequately and merely tries to ignore it?

Q1) What is the worst stress you've ever experienced?

Q2) What are your current stresses? How do you manage them?

# Express Yourself Directly

1. Rate the following situations on a scale of 10 (high stress) to 1 (no stress at all). Explain your answers.
   a) You just lost your job.
   b) You are divorced.
   c) Your kids' grades are falling.
   d) You got a traffic ticket.
   e) Your mortgage rate is going up.
   f) It's raining all day.
   g) You had an argument with your significant other.
   h) Your taxes are going up.
   i) You're gaining weight.
   j) You caught a cold.
   k) Your pet died.

# Let's Talk Funny

## The Only Way Left

A married couple are meeting a counselor to discuss their problems.

**Husband**: You know, every day the cost of living is rapidly rising. Our finances are becoming quite tight. I want to know how to cope with this problem.

**Counselor**: Simple. You should make more money or spend less.

**Husband**: I can't make any more money. I work as hard as I can, right now.

**Wife**: And I can't spend any less. All I ever buy are absolute necessities, like food and medical care.

**Husband**: Isn't there any solution?

**Counselor**: Only one, I'm afraid. You can STOP LIVING.

## Questions

(1) These days, inflation is a real problem. How do you cope with it?

(2) Which is easier? Making more money or spending less?

# What Does It Mean?

1

The time to relax is when you don't have time for it.

2

There's going to be stress in life, but it's your choice whether you let it affect you or not.

3

Pressure and stress are the common colds of the psyche.

4

God didn't do it all in one day. What makes me think I can?

5

Stress should be a powerful driving force, not an obstacle.

These expressions are related to the topics in this chapter. It will be good speaking practice to let students explain what these sentences mean in their own words in English.

**6**

When you find yourself stressed out, ask yourself one question: Will this matter in 5 years? If yes, then do something about the situation. If no, then let it go.

**7**

In the middle of the difficulty lies the opportunity.

**8**

Tension is who you think you should be. Relaxation is who you are.

**9**

For the sake of getting a living, men forget to live.

**10**

It is not just being overweight that's dangerous. Stress is also dangerous.

1

Too many people drown in the sea of stress because they neglect to wear a life jacket.

2

— I need a new line of work. This one is too stressful.
— Please don't change. If you quit, I'll be out of a job.
— Then let me go, and you can try to catch me again. That way we can both be employed.

10

I've had enough. You win.

You can't quit. I'm not through with you yet.

Think of these cartoons as scenes in a movie. The dialog has been scripted. Now we need actors to play the parts.

9

It can't get any more stressful than this. I feel like I'm going to explode.

I think I can balance my stress and my goal.

I'm perfectly happy because I have no stress, no job, no wife, NO ambition.

8

For weeks before I proposed, I was under a lot of stress. I didn't know what to say or do. And then, when I finally popped the question, she said NO.

For years I was under constant stress. Men kept asking me to marry them, and it was hard to keep saying NO.

3

4

S·Y·N·O·P·S·I·S

These are the pictures you've seen in this chapter. It will be good speaking practice for you to talk about these pictures once again. Your teacher will ask you "What are they doing?" or "What does this picture mean?" or some other question. You can give a straight answer or you can use your imagination. The purpose is to allow free conversation; there is no "right" answer.

S·Y·N·O·P·S·I·S

S·Y·N·O·P·S·I·S

5

7

6

The signs were clear, but I was in too much of a hurry to pay any attention.

12

Relaxation and peace of mind work against stress better than any insecticide against bugs.

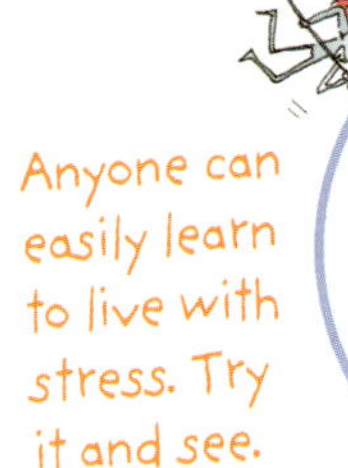

Anyone can easily learn to live with stress. Try it and see.

There's a lot to do. Get busy. Hurry up!

20

I refuse to worry about my weight. A fat man can be happy, but a worried man can never.

Think of these cartoons as scenes in a movie. The dialog has been scripted. Now we need actors to play the parts.

19

Whoever invented the concept of multitasking never had to do anything else.

18

— I'm content to be myself, though I know I won't ever get very far.
— I have to keep putting a lot of effort into it so I can go higher and faster.
— But no matter how far out you go, you always end up back where you started.

13

I have to keep stress and pressure on a short leash or they will end up crapping all over my life.

14

A few drops of water a day will make my flower bloom. But a whole bucketful will simply drown it.

## S·Y·N·O·P·S·I·S

These are the pictures you've seen in this chapter. It will be good speaking practice for you to talk about these pictures once again. Your teacher will ask you "What are they doing?" or "What does this picture mean?" or some other question. You can give a straight answer or you can use your imagination. The purpose is to allow free conversation; there is no "right" answer.

S·Y·N·O·P·S·I·S

S·Y·N·O·P·S·I·S

15

I keep trying to outrun stress, but the harder I run the sooner it catches up.

17

After crawling in darkness for decades, I finally saw the light.

16

The experts claim the next four years will be the most stressful in our history.

I want to find out if I'll be alive in five years. If not, I might as well start smoking and drinking while I can.

I just want to see what the future is going to be like.

If I know what's going to happen, I can make the best investments.

I want to see if my husband will still love me in five years.

Huh? I thought this was the line for the new STAR WARS movie.

# For Better Relationships

## Pictures Talk

1

Q1) Before you love others, you must love yourself first. Do you agree? Why or why not?

Q2) So, you say you love yourself? Prove it!

Q1) Little things that we do often seem to be the most important ways to develop good relationships. Talk about the little things that foster good relations.

Q2) What are the big things in defining relationship?

3

Q1) If you want to have a good reputation, should you praise others or criticize them? Why? Does the answer depend on circumstances?

Q2) Do ordinary people tend to praise others or to find fault with them?

Q1) What's a real friend?

Q2) How many real friends do you have? Should you be worried if you have just a few? Is it possible to have too many?

We are defined by our relationships. In isolation, in our own minds, we can be anyone we imagine, but our actual behavior and attitude toward others is all that we can be judged by. And, in the end, we are treated largely the same way we treat others. So it is in our own best interest to pay close attention to how we deal with others.

5

Q1) What are the most important things to maintain a friendship?

Q2) What are some good ways to make up with estranged friends? Or are they lost forever?

6

Q1) Can a man and a woman be real friends? Why or why not?

Q2) If your sweetheart wants to be friends with someone of the opposite sex, would you accept that? Why or why not?

7

Q1) What's the difference between the friends of your school days and those of your workplace?

Q2) Who is your most important friend at present? Talk about him or her.

8

Q1) The relationship between grown-up children and their parents is often not as good as we think it should be. Can you explain why?

Q2) What's the ideal relationship between young kids and their parents?

# Express Yourself Directly

1. Some say occasional quarrels among couples or friends make their relationship healthier. Do you agree or disagree? Why?
2. Why do some women put up with toxic boyfriends? And vice versa?
3. Everybody has a different mind-set. What's the best way to understand the viewpoints of others?
4. He says, "I don't like people. Instead, I have pets. They never betray my trust in them. They're my real friends." What kind of person is he? Describe his personality.
5. Some people try to take advantage of their relationships with others. How do they do so? Is that behavior wrong or understandable?

We need to check each other because we can't check ourselves.

# Let's Talk Funny

## The Successful Life

**Man**: Do you know the secret of a successful life?

**Friend**: No, I wish I did. What is it?

**Man**: You need to learn to say YES.

**Friend**: What do you mean?

**Man**: Whenever your SWEETHEART ASKS you to do something, you should say "Yes." Whenever your WIFE ADVISES you to do something, you must tell her, "Of course." And when your BOSS ORDERS you to do something, you should say "Definitely."

## Questions

(1) Do you agree with the man? Why or why not?

(2) How do you think lovers change over time? Is there any difference between being a sweetheart and being a spouse?

A safe relationship depends on a combination of three responses : "Yes," "Definitely," and "Of course." There is no place for "No" or "Maybe."

# What Does It Mean?

1

Remember, we all stumble, every one of us. That's why it's a comfort to walk hand in hand.

2

Assumptions are the termites of relationships.

3

When something is missing in your life, it usually turns out to be someone.

4

If fame were based on kindness instead of popularity, on understanding instead of attention, you should be the biggest celebrity on earth.

5

Lots of people want to ride with you in a limo, but what you really want is someone to share the bus with you if the limo breaks down.

These expressions are related to the topics in this chapter. It will be good speaking practice to let students explain what these sentences mean in their own words in English.

6

I just broke up with someone, and the last thing she said to me was, "You'll never find anyone like me again!" I hope she's right!

7

People are lonely because they build walls instead of bridges.

8

With good company, no road is long.

9

To know when to go away and when to come closer is the key to any lasting relationship.

10

Don't ask me what I think of you; I might not give you the answer you want.

1

I love myself so much that I want to disguise my face so I look like someone else.

2

I call this truck "Our Relationship" because it carries everything we have collected as a family.

The things themselves are not valuable. Some of them are broken.

But I don't understand. You should call it "Our Relation Truck."

After all, it's not a ship.

10

A safe relationship depends on a combination of three responses : "Yes," "Definitely," and "Of course." There is no place for "No" or "Maybe."

**Think of these cartoons as scenes in a movie. The dialog has been scripted. Now we need actors to play the parts.**

9

We need to check each other because we can't check ourselves.

8

This hurts me more than it will hurt you.

Then let's reverse roles and neither of us will feel so bad.

3

Are you finished examining me with a magnifying glass?

Why are you asking me to hurry up? Do you have something to hide?

4

I guess we're nearing the end of our journey together.

I hope the road ahead of us is longer than the one behind us. After all, this is only our first date.

## S · Y · N · O · P · S · I · S

These are the pictures you've seen in this chapter. It will be good speaking practice for you to talk about these pictures once again. Your teacher will ask you "What are they doing?" or "What does this picture mean?" or some other question. You can give a straight answer or you can use your imagination. The purpose is to allow free conversation; there is no "right" answer.

S · Y · N · O · P · S · I · S

S · Y · N · O · P · S · I · S

5

I wish we could be even closer than we are.

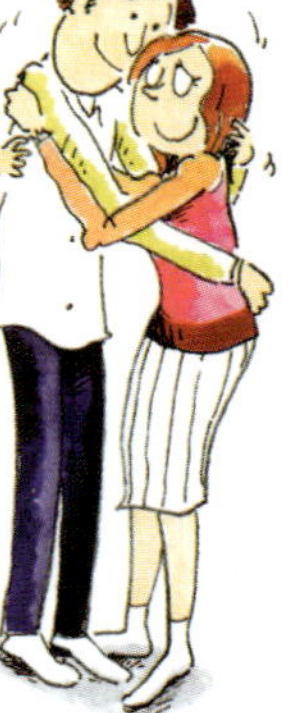

You already are at the center of my being. How could we get any closer than that?

7

You two are much older than any of my other friends.

You're the only real friends I have who are female.

I always wondered why people would say I shouldn't be friends with my children or husband. If we weren't all best friends, how could we share any other roles?

6

You're my best friend. I think we should get married.

You're my best friend too. Why spoil a good relationship by changing it into something else?

Hold my hand, Dear.

Hang on tight.

Thank you for helping me. I don't walk as good as I used to.

Will you swing me? It feels like flying.

12

I used to assume that all boys are terrible people. Then I met my boyfriend, who always seems so nice and perfect. I hope my assumptions about him are not as false as the ones I used to have.

20

Being married is a constant test.

The problem is, all the answers are wrong.

Think of these cartoons as scenes in a movie. The dialog has been scripted. Now we need actors to play the parts.

19

Every time I'm at one end of my swing, you seem like you're on the other end.

Why don't we both stop in the middle?

18

It feels like we've walked a continent together.

I'm sorry that you feel that way. To me it was like a stroll in the park.

13

— Hey, sweetheart, are you having fun?
— What are you doing here? I took this vacation to try to get away from you.
— But, whether you want me to be there or not, I'll always be in your thoughts.
— If that's the case, I might as well go home.

14

No bicycle can go if either tire goes flat.

## S·Y·N·O·P·S·I·S

These are the pictures you've seen in this chapter. It will be good speaking practice for you to talk about these pictures once again. Your teacher will ask you "What are they doing?" or "What does this picture mean?" or some other question. You can give a straight answer or you can use your imagination. The purpose is to allow free conversation; there is no "right" answer.

S·Y·N·O·P·S·I·S

15

— How did you get this flat tire?
— I didn't pay any attention to the road sign.
— What road sign?
— The one that said, "SHARP TURN AHEAD."
— But how did your tire go flat making a turn?
— You don't understand. I ran over the sign.

17

Tomorrow I'll bring an awl to work so I can make a hole in the partition between us.

Why? Do you want to spy on me?

16

Some day you'll be sorry you left me!

Maybe. I'm already sorry I met you.

# Issue 15 Money

## Pictures Talk

1

Q1) Every day, how often do you think about money? Is money important in your life? Why or why not?

Q2) What's the easiest way to make a fortune?

2

Q1) How much do you save every month? Is that enough to live on when you no longer work?

Q2) Talk about ways you can save money.

3

Q1) Is saving money any fun? Why or why not?

Q2) How can we make saving money more fun?

4

Q1) Is there any way you can increase your income? How?

Q2) What about ways you can cut spending? Is it easy?

That old man looks like a million dollars, green and wrinkled! The young man, on the other hand, shines like a penny. This just goes to show that money, in and of itself, is not the most important thing in the world, and is far less important than health, ability, attitude, and relationships.

5

Q1) Some say, "I can't save a penny!" Do you believe them?

Q2) Some say, "I save no money; it's nonsense to save in the face of this everlasting inflation." Do you agree or disagree?

6

Q1) Kids are getting too expensive; it requires a fortune to be spent on them until they are on their own. Do you think raising kids is worth the money? Why or why not?

Q2) Some people choose to remain childless because of finances. Can you understand their attitude? Or do you think everyone should have kids regardless of financial status?

7

Q1) The rich are getting richer. Is it therefore just to impose higher taxes on them? Why or why not?

Q2) If the wealth gap between the rich and poor continues to widen, what do you think will happen?

8

Q1) How much do you need for your retirement? How can you get the money you need?

Q2) If that method is a long shot, what are other options available?

# Express Yourself Directly

1. What are the good things and bad things associated with having too much money?
2. If a car costs $20,000 today and the same car is expected to be 20% less a year from now, would you buy it now or later?
3. Money begets money. How?
4. Money is said to be the root of vice. Do you agree or disagree? Why?
5. Some millionaires think they're not rich because they are not billionaires, and some poorer people regard themselves as rich because they have three meals a day. What's the difference between their attitudes? Who's right?

I never thought it was possible to drown in money.

# Let's Talk Funny

## Getting Over Money Worries

**Man**: Making money is hard but spending it is easy. Why? It's not fair.

**Friend**: I disagree.

**Man**: Why?

**Friend**: For me, spending money is a lot more difficult than making it.

**Man**: Come on, you must be kidding!

**Friend**: No, I'm dead serious.

**Man**: Tell me what you mean.

**Friend**: I have always made money, but since I got married my wife hasn't allowed me to spend any. So I've FORGOTTEN how to do it.

## Questions

(1) Do you think the man is happy? Why or why not?

(2) Which is easier in your case, making money or spending it?

He doesn't know how to spend his money wisely, so he buries it. But he can't bury his problems.

# What Does It Mean?

1

If you want to feel rich, just count the things you have that money can't buy.

2

Money is not the most important thing in the world. Love is. But, fortunately for me, I love money.

3

Money often costs too much.

4

Don't tell me what your priorities are. Show me where you spend your money and I'll tell you what they are.

5

Make money your god and it will plague you like the devil.

These expressions are related to the topics in this chapter. It will be good speaking practice to let students explain what these sentences mean in their own words in English.

6

The easiest way for your children to learn about money is for you not to have any.

7

The safest way to double your money is to fold it over and put it in your pocket.

8

Money can't buy happiness, but neither can poverty.

9

No matter how rich you become, how famous or how powerful, when you die the size of your funeral will still pretty much depend on the weather.

10

If you want to know the value of money, try to borrow some.

1

In my mind, time is always money.

2

I don't understand. I thought the bank was there to KEEP my money, not TAKE it.

10

He doesn't know how to spend his money wisely, so he buries it. But he can't bury his problems.

**Think of these cartoons as scenes in a movie. The dialog has been scripted. Now we need actors to play the parts.**

9

I never thought it was possible to drown in money.

8

The difference between us is this : A squirrel saves nuts for the future, but you are nuts because you don't save anything for the future.

I used to think that was a squirrelly philosophy, but now I know better. If I could only start over.

3

Nowadays it's cheaper to build a house out of money than to buy the bricks.

4

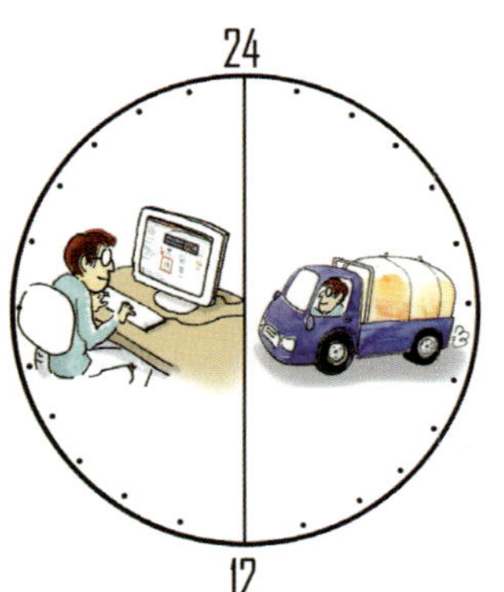


All day I work in the office, but I still have to drive a truck at night. And the bonus is, I have no time left to spend money.

S·Y·N·O·P·S·I·S

These are the pictures you've seen in this chapter. It will be good speaking practice for you to talk about these pictures once again. Your teacher will ask you "What are they doing?" or "What does this picture mean?" or some other question. You can give a straight answer or you can use your imagination. The purpose is to allow free conversation; there is no "right" answer.

S·Y·N·O·P·S·I·S

5

I tried to save for a rainy day, but I hadn't planned on a typhoon.

So far I've managed to avoid all temptations to spend my money on foolish things.

I was taught that a penny saved is a penny earned, but nobody told me in today's world I needed dollars.

7

It's too bad you couldn't afford a parachute.

If you hadn't crashed the plane I wouldn't need one.

6

The heavier the kid grows, the more it costs.

I wonder how much the sun costs, but I get it for free. Who lets me breathe the fresh air, who allows me to smell the flowers? It's a great place to be, even with no money.

12

I'm sincere, honest, and fun to be with. Why don't you love me?

You have everything to make a girl happy. Except for one thing....

I'm fat and cold and unfeeling, but I get the girl every time.

20

It's simple. I have money, and you want money. If you're not interested in my terms, then I still have it and you still want it. It's up to you.

But I don't want to buy your money. I only want to rent it for a little while.

Think of these cartoons as scenes in a movie. The dialog has been scripted. Now we need actors to play the parts.

19

This is the first funeral I went to that nobody came. Not even the driver.

This is the last time I plan a party without stipulating RSVP.

18

Climbing after happiness is a lot harder than I thought. I already have money. So maybe I have enough to be happy.

You can quit if you want, but I don't have any. So I can't stop now.

13

We all get rolled over by the economy once in a while.

14

Sell me a chance to get rich, even though I know he odds are almost impossible.

Carefully saving my money is a sure way to get richer.

S·Y·N·O·P·S·I·S

These are the pictures you've seen in this chapter. It will be good speaking practice for you to talk about these pictures once again. Your teacher will ask you "What are they doing?" or "What does this picture mean?" or some other question. You can give a straight answer or you can use your imagination. The purpose is to allow free conversation; there is no "right" answer.

S·Y·N·O·P·S·I·S

S·Y·N·O·P·S·I·S

15

I should have worshipped beauty.

17

I'm glad I bought my new safe. They told me it was unbreakable.

My uncle made another sale and gave me the combination so we both made out.

16

I'm poor so you can learn the value of money. My own father was rich, so I never learned.

I wish I lived with grandpa.

# Smoking & Drinking

## Pictures Talk

Q1) Do you believe somebody who claims, "I'm a social drinker?" Give your reasons.

Q2) Why isn't anybody a "social smoker"?

2

Q1) Do you think drinking helps cultivate socially viable relationships? Why or why not? What about smoking?

Q2) Give some examples of drinking or smoking backfiring in a social setting.

Q1) Why are juvenile smoking and drinking on the rise? Talk about ways of curbing them.

Q2) Many youngsters say they won't quit smoking because they are afraid of gaining weight. Is that a good reason or just an excuse?

Q1) What are some common excuses smokers and drinkers use when they can't quit?

Q2) Some people say their job "forces" them to smoke and drink. Do you believe them?

I once had a friend who was a chain smoker. He couldn't last 10 minutes without a cigarette. He had to forego many events because they were no-smoking affairs. He couldn't fly, though he loved to travel. It became increasingly difficult to eat in a nice restaurant. Even bars began to exclude him. His "habit" cost him a sizeable percentage of his income every year. He tried to quit, many times, but he was never successful. Eventually, he developed a hacking cough, high blood pressure, and heart and lung problems that were all associated with his addiction. "I don't smoke," he once complained to me. "The cigarette smokes." Then he gave me the saddest look I've ever seen." I'm just the sucker at the other end."

5

Q1) Do you think spouses have a right to say "no" to their partners' smoking and drinking? Why or why not?

Q2) What would you do if your kids asked you to stop smoking and drinking? Would you say "Yes" or "Mind your own business"?

6

Q1) Do you see any difference between men smoking and women smoking? Give your reasons.

Q2) Is there any difference between women's drinking and men's drinking? Why or why not?

7

Q1) Could we reduce the number of smokers by sharply increasing the price of tobacco? Why or why not?

Q2) Can "sin taxes" (special taxes on vices such as smoking, drinking, or gambling wins) be justified? If so, how?

8

Q1) Do you think employers are entitled to refuse to hire smokers or drinkers, especially if the employers are responsible for providing health insurance?

Q2) What if you were pressured to choose between no-smoking and the pink slip? What would you do?

# Express Yourself Directly

1. Is our society responsible for young people smoking and drinking? Why or why not? Answer in detail.
2. Should those who smoke or drink pay a health premium in the form of higher taxes or insurance payments? Why or why not? What about those who don't exercise, or those who don't take their prescription medicine?
3. Should smokers and drinkers be discriminated against when they try to get a job or a promotion? Should they be promoted more easily? Should it be an irrelevant factor? Explain your answer.
4. The government permits the sale of tobacco and liquor, but it criminalizes the sale of many kinds of drugs. Why? Is the government morally right?
5. Smoking is prohibited on the street in some cities. Are you for or against this ban?
6. What do you think about our own drinking culture, especially in comparison to others?
7. When some people get into serious trouble, they say, "Sorry, I was drunk when I did it." Is that a good justification for their actions?

## Living in the Republic of Lawsuits

This country is becoming the Republic of Lawsuits. Fat people are suing fast food chains for making them that way. Drivers charged with causing an accident go to court to prove that it was due to a malfunction of their car and demand compensation from the manufacturer. Smokers are suing cigarette makers for their lung cancer. One drunkard was reportedly ready to sue liquor companies until he learned that the smokers were not winning their cases. So he changed his mind and instead decided to sue Bacchus — THE GOD OF WINE.

## Questions

(1) What does the Republic of Lawsuits mean?

(2) Do you think it is reasonable for smokers to sue cigarette manufactures? What about obese people suing fast food companies?

# What Does It Mean?

1

It's easy to quit smoking. I've done it hundreds of times.

2

The best way to stop smoking is to just stop — no ifs, ands, or buts.

3

One thousand Americans stop smoking every day — by dying.

4

Nicotine patches are great. If you stick one over each eye, you can't find your cigarettes.

5

The best way to stop smoking is to carry wet matches.

These expressions are related to the topics in this chapter. It will be good speaking practice to let students explain what these sentences mean in their own words in English.

6

Alcohol may be man's worst enemy, but many religions say you should love your enemy.

7

I went on a diet, swore off drinking and smoking, and in fourteen days I lost two weeks.

8

Explain why these are oxymorons.

- Responsible drinking
- Healthy smoking
- Selfless politician
- Military intelligence

Responsible drinking? That's an oxymoron.

I envy people who drink. At least they have something to blame everything on. And when they get sick, at least they can get better by giving up something.

A drunk was in front of a judge. The judge says, "You have been brought here for drinking." The drunk says, "Okay, let's get started."

1

— Some people drink to be happy.
— Some drink to forget.
— But I don't know what I have to be happy about.
— And I forgot what it was that I wanted to forget.
— Cheers!

2

What do you want to do when you leave? How about going to my place?

No thanks. The first thing I expect to do is get sick and then become unconscious. I'd better do that at home.

10

I drink to get high. But I never wanted to get THIS high!

Think of these cartoons as scenes in a movie. The dialog has been scripted. Now we need actors to play the parts.

9

Do you take this bottle to be your constant companion, through sickness and in health, till death do you part?

8

— I'm glad they don't mention alcoholics.
— It's hard to choose between my need to smoke and my need to work.
— Not fair! Without a job I can't afford to buy cigarettes.
— If I have no money, I'll stop smoking. So then I can get a job and be able to smoke again.

3

– Smoke these. They taste great and they will help you lose weight.
– Then maybe I would be invited out to more parties.
– Of course! And please contact me when you need to buy some liquor too.

4

I need to remind myself of why I can't quit smoking and drinking.

## S·Y·N·O·P·S·I·S

These are the pictures you've seen in this chapter. It will be good speaking practice for you to talk about these pictures once again. Your teacher will ask you "What are they doing?" or "What does this picture mean?" or some other question. You can give a straight answer or you can use your imagination. The purpose is to allow free conversation; there is no "right" answer.

S·Y·N·O·P·S·I·S

S·Y·N·O·P·S·I·S

5

It's bad enough that you nag me at home. Do you have to also organize a street demonstration against your dad?

7

The cost of cigarettes keeps rising, but the cost of narcotics is on the decline. Maybe I should consider switching.

6

Honey, whatever you do, I'll do it with you.

That's good. Can you help me drive? We're both almost half conscious, I guess, so 1/2 + 1/2=1

11

Some people schedule in advance the day they will quit smoking and the day they will resume.

12

If I were sick I'd stop smoking. And I would feel better. But then I could start again.

20

You're charged with driving while being legally drunk.

If it was legal, how can that be a crime?

Think of these cartoons as scenes in a movie. The dialog has been scripted. Now we need actors to play the parts.

19

I collect bottles. The best part of my hobby is that before I collect them I get to empty them into my body.

18

Explain why these are oxymorons.

- Responsible drinking
- Healthy smoking
- Selfless politician
- Military intelligence

Oxy is short for oxygen. A moron is a stupid person. Does this mean that breathing makes us dumb?

**13**

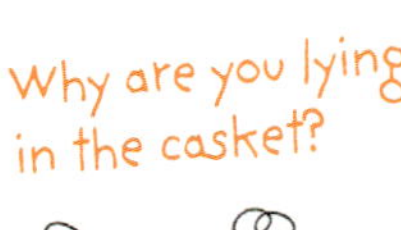

I'm just seeing what it would be like if I didn't smoke anymore.

**14**

Sometimes it's better if I can't watch what I'm doing to myself.

## S·Y·N·O·P·S·I·S

These are the pictures you've seen in this chapter. It will be good speaking practice for you to talk about these pictures once again. Your teacher will ask you "What are they doing?" or "What does this picture mean?" or some other question. You can give a straight answer or you can use your imagination. The purpose is to allow free conversation; there is no "right" answer.

S·Y·N·O·P·S·I·S

S·Y·N·O·P·S·I·S

**15**

While I'm looking for a CAMEL to smoke, I might as well make sure my matches are dry.

**16**

I believe we should fill our space with things that make us happy.

**17**

Habits are too strong to break, and the hammer of determination is too fragile.

# Issue 17 Who Do You Trust & Not Trust?

## Pictures Talk

1

Q1) Do you trust your friends? How much?

Q2) Would you still trust them if money were involved? Why or why not?

2

Q1) Do you trust your spouse unconditionally?

Q2) Do you ever see your trust eroding? What would you do in that situation?

3

Q1) Do you trust your neighbors?

Q2) How can you tell if they are trustworthy or not?

4

Q1) Do you trust your boss? Do you have good reason for your attitude?

Q2) How can you make your boss have more trust in you?

*Once, when I was in serious financial difficulty, I was surprised when someone I hardly knew, and who I thought disliked me, offered me an interest-free loan until I got back onto my feet. In a few months, I was able to pay him back, but we never did develop a close relationship. Later on, an old friend of mine found himself in similar straits, and I loaned him a large sum of money to help him out. But, to this very day, he has not even attempted to pay me back. I think it is odd that a near-stranger correctly trusted me to do the right thing, while a trusted friend betrayed my faith in him.*

Q1) Do you trust weather reports?

Q2) Why aren't weathermen fired even after making a string of wrong forecasts?

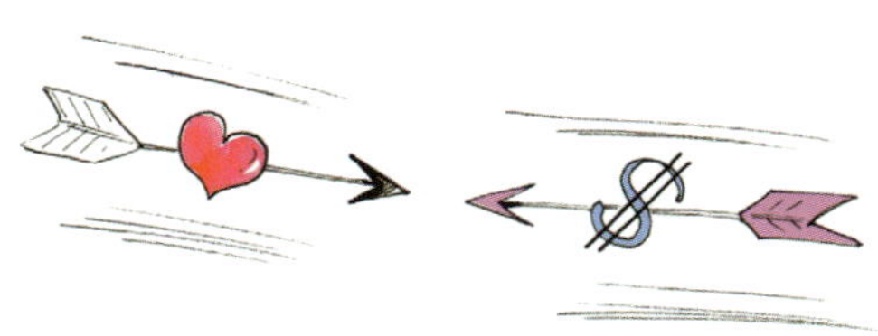

Q1) Do you believe in the power of money? Why or why not?

Q2) Does the power of love ever outperform the power of money? Can you give any examples?

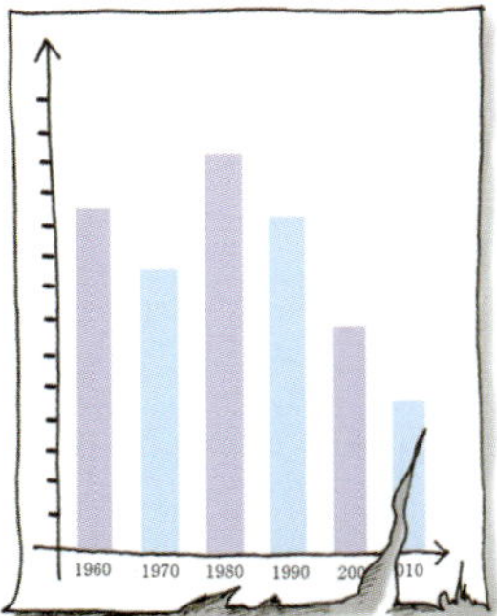


Q1) Do you trust government statistics such as the price index, the unemployment rate, or the growth rate? Why or why not?

Q2) Do you believe the government will actually pay you the pension that is due to you?

Q1) Does religion play its expected role in your life? Why or why not?

Q2) Does your faith bring peace to you? Or does it make you feel anxious?

# Express Yourself Directly

1. Rate the following professionals on a scale of 10 (trusted completely) to 1 (not trusted at all) and tell why.
   a) doctors
   b) lawyers and judges
   c) firefighters
   d) police
   e) politicians
   f) stock brokers
   g) teachers
   h) religious leaders
   i) government officials
   j) real estate agents
   k) fortune-tellers
   l) panhandlers
   m) car salesmen
   n) matchmakers
   o) business people

# Let's Talk Funny

## He & She

1. He's just rich enough to help only himself. She's not rich at all, but she's always ready to share half her bread with the poor.
2. He's just intelligent enough to avoid legal responsibility for his actions. She's not very intelligent, but she fulfills all her moral and legal obligations.
3. He's generous enough to forgive himself. She's generous enough to forgive everyone except herself.
4. He uses his popularity to take advantage of others. She's popular too, but she uses her charm to help those who are unpopular.
5. A powerful man, he threatens the weak. She uses her power to help them.
6. He's handsome and uses his good looks to attract women. She's beautiful but wants to be judged only by her ability.
7. He climbs mountains so he can brag that he's a mountain climber. She hikes in the mountains just because she likes to.
8. He boasts about his physical strength and ridicules the feeble-minded. She is physically handicapped but helps people who are mentally handicapped.
9. He reads books in order to make money. She reads them to enrich her life.
10. He's sure he knows the WORLD, but she knows a little about LIFE.

I may not be rich, but I have many people in my life.

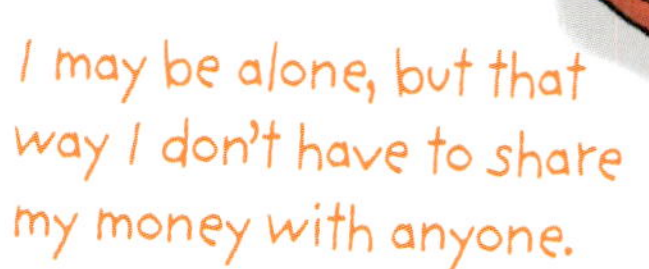


## Questions

(1) What's the difference between him and her?

(2) Which one represents most people, do you think? What's your own type?

# What Does It Mean?

1

Trust is like a vase. Once it's broken, even though you can fix it, the vase will never be the same.

2

Where large sums of money are concerned, it is advisable to trust nobody.

3

All you need in this life is honesty and confidence; then success is sure.

4

I would rather trust a woman's instinct than a man's reason.

5

Never trust the advice of a man in difficulties.

6

There are only two ways to live. One is as though nothing is a miracle, and the other is as if everything is.

7

Be faithful in small things because it is in them that your strength lies.

8

Faith can move mountains, but don't be surprised if God hands you a shovel.

9

A skeptic is a person who would ask God for his ID card.

10

We're all born brave, trusting, and greedy; most of us remain greedy.

1

Too often, money comes between good friends.

Well, if you walk away it won't be between us anymore.

2

I can always trust you to pick a fight with me!

I can always trust you to give me a reason to pick a fight.

10

I may not be rich, but I have many people in my life.

I may be alone, but that way I don't have to share my money with anyone.

Think of these cartoons as scenes in a movie. The dialog has been scripted. Now we need actors to play the parts.

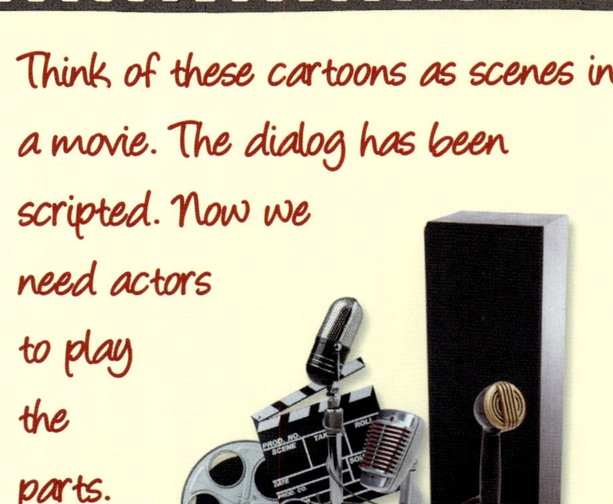

9

Why are my talents and abilities not better appreciated?

You do what you enjoy doing, but I just work to make money. Because I'm rich, others automatically give me a high rating.

8

When the boat is sinking and people pray, how can they be certain the others are praying to the wrong god?

3

4

## S·Y·N·O·P·S·I·S

These are the pictures you've seen in this chapter. It will be good speaking practice for you to talk about these pictures once again. Your teacher will ask you "What are they doing?" or "What does this picture mean?" or some other question. You can give a straight answer or you can use your imagination. The purpose is to allow free conversation; there is no "right" answer.

S·Y·N·O·P·S·I·S

5

6

7

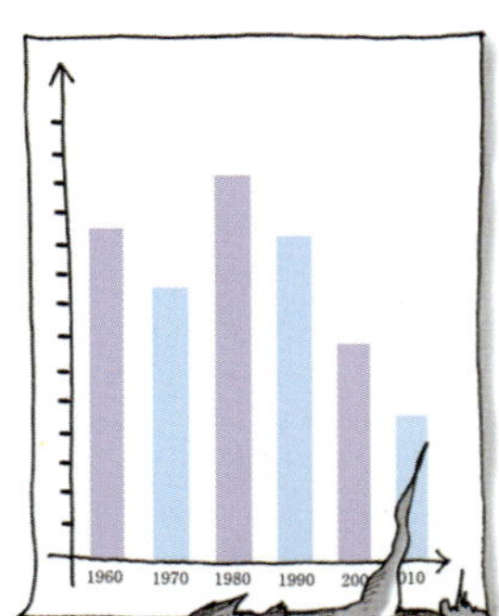

11

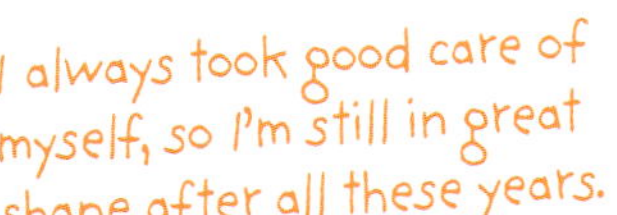

I just never thought I would be around this long, so I never bothered to take care of myself. But I had a great time.

12

Winner take all!!

If you let me win, I'll let you have some of it.

20

I can't be greedy, or I would want all the bags.

Think of these cartoons as scenes in a movie. The dialog has been scripted. Now we need actors to play the parts.

19

I need to see your birth certificate.

Why do you bother? In three days I'll have another one.

18

If I had prayed for an answer, I guess God would have given me a library card.

13

Why does success keep eluding me? Maybe I picked the wrong bike.

14

I don't know why I know but still I know.

You can't be sure. I planned it too carefully.

S·Y·N·O·P·S·I·S

These are the pictures you've seen in this chapter. It will be good speaking practice for you to talk about these pictures once again. Your teacher will ask you "What are they doing?" or "What does this picture mean?" or some other question. You can give a straight answer or you can use your imagination. The purpose is to allow free conversation; there is no "right" answer.

S·Y·N·O·P·S·I·S

S·Y·N·O·P·S·I·S

15

Buy now. The market is ready to take off.

That's what you said before you dug yourself in a hole.

16

My life has always been one easy triumph after another.

You're just lucky. For me, no matter what I do, it's been a never-ending series of disasters.

17

No matter how many precautions we take, there is always some risk, even when riding a tricycle.

# Issue 18 Tie the Knot or Not— That Is the Question

## Pictures Talk

**1**

Q1) Do you think tying the knot is a must? Why or why not?

Q2) Why do some people get married and others remain single?

**2**

Q1) Some people say getting married is nonsense. What do you think they mean?

Q2) How do married people regard single people, and vice versa? Can they understand each other? Do you think they envy or hate each other?

**3**

Q1) What would your ideal spouse be like? Is there anyone you know who meets those particular qualifications?

Q2) Which is more important in marriage, money or love?

**4**

Q1) Do you think your future spouse must have a job? Does it have to pay well? Why or why not?

Q2) If your spouse lost his or her job, would you consider a divorce?

Not long ago, being married was an almost universal norm. Single adults were considered eccentric at best, outcasts at worst. But, while most people still get married eventually, it is increasingly common for people to delay marriage or avoid it entirely, even as the ones who get married tend to stay that way for shorter periods of time and to marry more often.

5

Q1) Do you want to have kids? If so, how many? If not, why not?

Q2) Would you consider adopting? Why or why not?

6

Q1) Is it okay to live together before getting married? Why or why not?

Q2) What would happen if living together didn't work out? What would happen if people married each other without living together first, and then found they were incompatible?

7

Q1) They say an ideal date is different from an ideal spouse. Agree or disagree?

Q2) Is it okay to have friends of the opposite sex after you get married?

8

Q1) Do you believe a lot of gold diggers exist?

Q2) What if a person marries someone much older but with a lot of money and claims, "It's real love"? Do you believe that person?

# Express Yourself Directly

1. It is said that marriage is not a matter just between the couple themselves, but between all family members. What does that mean?
2. Do you think a prenuptial agreement is a good idea? Why or why not?
3. Do you think the in-laws' financial status should be an important factor in someone's marriage choice? Why or why not?
4. Kids are getting more and more expensive. What do you think the government should do to help a large family?
5. Describe the ideal marriage.
6. Divorce is on the rise. Do you think that situation is really a big deal? Why or why not?

# Let's Talk Funny

## The Perfect Marriage

**Counselor**: What can I do to help you?

**Lady**: My husband is a workaholic. I seldom see him.

**Counselor**: Do you want to get a divorce?

**Lady**: No way!

**Counselor**: Because you love him?

**Lady**: No. Absolutely not.

**Counselor**: Hmmmm. You rarely see him, you don't love him, but you don't want a divorce? Very strange!

**Lady**: You see, he makes a lot of money. I have an extremely agreeable lifestyle.

**Counselor**: Then what is it you want me to do?

**Lady**: I want to know how to keep this kind of marriage as LONG as I wish.

## Questions

(1) What would you think about having a rich workaholic as your spouse?

(2) Do marriage counselors prevent many divorces, or do they just make it easier for unhappy couples to separate?

# What Does It Mean?

1

When a man marries a woman, they become one — the trouble starts when they try to decide which one.

2

You never know anyone until you marry him (or her).

3

Sometimes I watch old couples in a restaurant eating their meals together. Sometimes they don't even talk to each other. Is it because they have nothing more to say, or can they simply read each other's mind by now?

4

Marriage is a three-ring circus — engagement ring, wedding ring, and suffering.

5

Keep your eyes open before marriage and half shut afterwards.

6

A successful marriage is an alliance entered into by a man who can't sleep with the window shut, and a woman who can't sleep with it open.

7

Never get married in the morning, because you never know who you'll meet that night.

8

In England, it is against the law for a man to marry his mother-in-law. In every other country, this is regarded as useless legislation.

9

As to marriage or celibacy, let a man take which course he will, he will be sure to repent.

10

I never knew what real happiness was until I got married. And then it was too late.

1

In which book will we find "prenup"?

I think it's in another book, "No Great Expectations."

2

Marriage is two people working together to reach the same goals.

Marriage is voluntarily giving up one's freedom to do whatever one pleases.

10

I hope you don't mind if I have to work during our vacation. I have a big deal that I have to close.

Oh, that's all right. Maybe you can do two big deals, and next year we can afford an even better holiday.

Think of these cartoons as scenes in a movie. The dialog has been scripted. Now we need actors to play the parts.

9

You're not just half of a couple. You're part of our entire family, spread over many generations.

I love my wife so I guess I have to pretend I care for my in-laws too.

8

I'm fortunate to have such a beautiful woman who loves me so much.

Can't that man see she's only interested in his money?

They say love is blind, but in this case it's the old, rich lover who's blind.

But you're an easy man to love — so kind and generous!

I just want to know why I'm stuck with a pair of losers like you. There must be another sweet rich guy somewhere.

S · Y · N · O · P · S · I · S

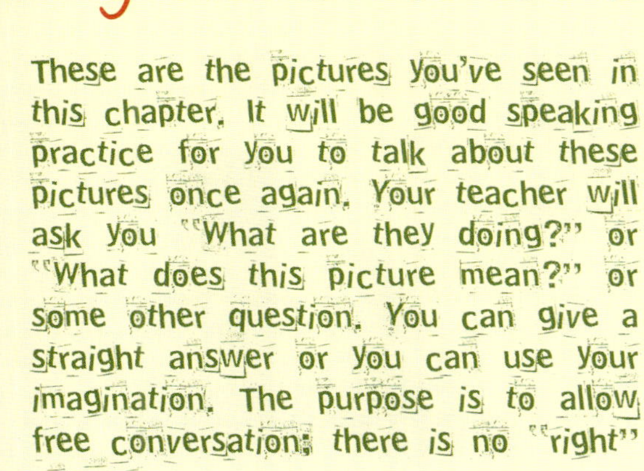

These are the pictures you've seen in this chapter. It will be good speaking practice for you to talk about these pictures once again. Your teacher will ask you "What are they doing?" or "What does this picture mean?" or some other question. You can give a straight answer or you can use your imagination. The purpose is to allow free conversation; there is no "right" answer.

11

How could I be so wrong about him? He's nothing but an egotist.

Before I married her, I wish I had known what she's really like.

20

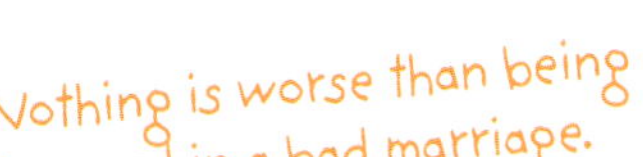

One thing is worse – being stuck in a bad marriage with you.

Think of these cartoons as scenes in a movie. The dialog has been scripted. Now we need actors to play the parts.

19

It doesn't matter which road I choose, I'll be sorry either way.

18

If you were my husband, I'd scratch your eyes out.

I'd have to be blind to be married to you in the first place.

If I were married to either one of you, I'd have to be a real cheddar head.

**13**

My husband! He's the same strong, quiet man he was when I married him.

Finally! It took 30 years for my wife to learn how to hold her tongue.

**14**

You'll never last 12 rounds with me. I'll knock you out in the 7th.

Before we married, you said I was a real knockout. But now I just want to knock your block off.

## S·Y·N·O·P·S·I·S

These are the pictures you've seen in this chapter. It will be good speaking practice for you to talk about these pictures once again. Your teacher will ask you "What are they doing?" or "What does this picture mean?" or some other question. You can give a straight answer or you can use your imagination. The purpose is to allow free conversation; there is no "right" answer.

S·Y·N·O·P·S·I·S

S·Y·N·O·P·S·I·S

**15**

You may kiss the bride.

My dad told me that his marriage was a real eye-opener. Afterwards, all the mystery and romance were gone from the world.

My mother told me I shouldn't get married without a blindfold. But I compromised and wore sunglasses instead.

**17**

I'm glad you could make it. I was so worried you wouldn't show.

I had another date, but she stood me up.

**16**

It doesn't matter if the window is open or closed. I can't sleep anyway because of his snoring.

I used to stay awake if the window were closed. But now, after listening to her nagging all these years, I can sleep through anything.

# Has Gender Equality Been Achieved?

## Pictures Talk

1

Q1) Do you think women are discriminated against when it comes to job-seeking? If so, how?

Q2) Talk about the kinds of discrimination men (and women) suffer in the workplace.

2

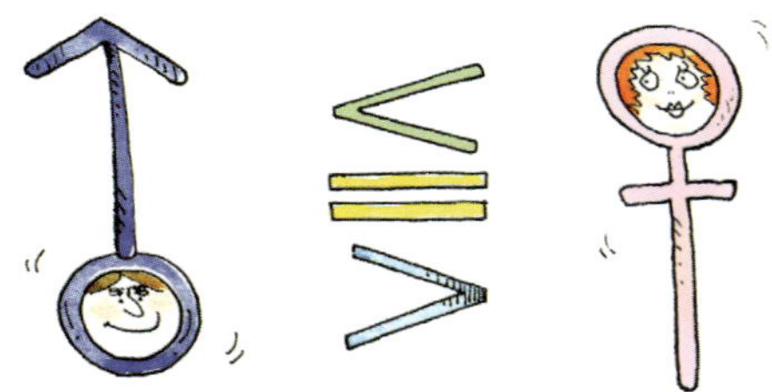

Q1) Do most families still prefer baby boys over girls? Why do you think so?

Q2) What about you?

3

Q1) Is it okay for your baby girl to behave like a tomboy?

Q2) The saying is that boys should be boys and girls should be girls. What does it mean?

4

Q1) Do you think household chores are for women only? Why or why not?

Q2) How does your family divvy up the chores?

For millennia, men have dominated (usually monopolized) positions of power, wealth, education, opportunity, status, and personal freedom. Occasionally, a woman has intruded into these male domains and, very infrequently, has even surpassed the men, but these situations have been regarded as anomalies. However, more and more, men are losing their grip on the situation, as more women rise higher in more fields. Are we approaching a period of sexual equality, or a time of female superiority?

5

Q1) Some say a college education for a woman is a waste of time and money. Refute them, or argue their case.

Q2) Is a college diploma really worthwhile for women who become stay-at-home moms? What about for househusbands?

6

Q1) What is your opinion of househusbands?

Q2) Would you consider becoming a househusband if your wife made more money than you? Would you want your husband to make that decision?

7

Q1) Do you think it's fair that only men are conscripted into military service?

Q2) What do you think about giving an advantage to job-seekers who have finished military service? Should they get any preferences in pay or promotions?

8

Q1) Among newlyweds, who is more powerful in everyday decisions, the husband or the wife? Does the situation change over time?

Q2) Who should be in charge in financial matters?

# Express Yourself Directly

1. Men still comprise most of the CEOs, political leaders, university presidents, and so forth. Does this mean that a glass ceiling actually exists or that relatively few women are actually qualified to hold these positions?
2. When it comes to downsizing, corporations are willing to rid female workers first. Does this show outright discrimination against women? Why or why not?
3. Some say if we elected a female president, our society would become more morally righteous because women are less corruptible than men. Agree or disagree?
4. Do you believe some form of violence against women still exists in our society? Explain your answer.
5. How do we protect women if society still thinks sexual harassment is a joke?
6. When is it possible to say we've reached a perfectly gender-equal society?

# Let's Talk Funny

## Because

1. I don't have to make money, because my wife has a job.
2. I don't help my wife with household chores, because I love her. They're good exercise for her.
3. I don't have to remember my wife's birthday because she always reminds me.
4. I try to overspend, because it encourages my wife to earn more money.
5. I am poor; I can only afford to have one car, one house, one vacation abroad per year, and only one million dollars in my account.
6. But I love my wife because she does EVERYTHING for me.

## Questions

(1) Do you think he is poor? Why or why not?

(2) Do you believe he really loves his wife? Why or why not?

# What Does It Mean?

1

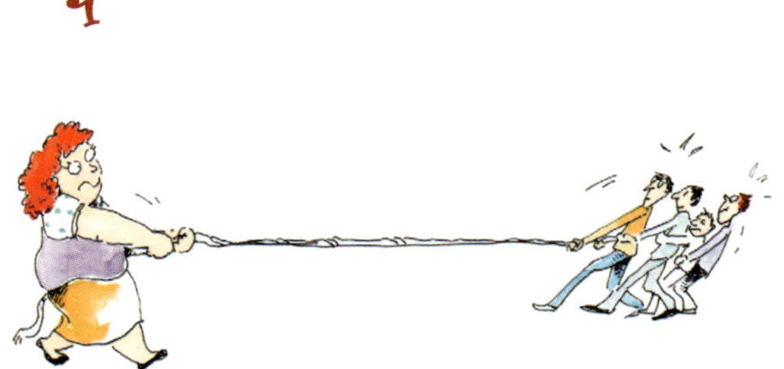

Being a woman is a terribly difficult task, since it principally consists of dealing with men.

2

I do not wish women to have power over men but over themselves.

3

It matters more what's in a woman's face than what's on it.

4

I would have girls regard themselves not as adjectives but as nouns.

5

Nobody objects to a woman being a good writer or sculptor or geneticist as long as she also manages to be a good wife, a good mother, a good-looking woman and good-tempered.

These expressions are related to the topics in this chapter. It will be good speaking practice to let students explain what these sentences mean in their own words in English.

6

Few men I can think of are as capable, as smart, as funny, as compassionate, and as remarkable — as most women.

7

The reason there are so few female politicians is that it is too much trouble to put makeup on two faces.

8

We have begun to raise daughters to be more like sons, but few of us have the courage to raise our sons to be more like our daughters.

9

A woman is like a tea bag. It's only when she's in hot water that you realize how strong she is.

10

Men aren't really the enemy — they are fellow victims suffering from an outmoded masculine mystique that makes them feel unnecessarily inadequate when there are no bears left to kill.

1

I expect you to work twice as hard as the gals in the office for half the salary and none of the benefits. Oh, and bring me a coffee.

Yes, ma'am. Right away.
(My boss at work treats me the same way as my wife at home)

2

Men are the kings of the world, with superior intelligence and ability.

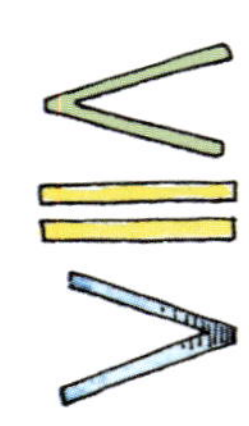

Women like men to think so, because that way it's easier for us to manipulate them.

10

Not many adult men are pampered like I am. I'm very lucky!

You poor little thing. Just let me take care of you and don't worry about a thing.

Why doesn't she take care of me? I should be in the baby buggy instead of him!

Think of these cartoons as scenes in a movie. The dialog has been scripted. Now we need actors to play the parts.

9

A good little woman is never outweighed by a bigger man.

8

If you promise to be a good boy, I'll let you have a little bit more money this week.

I promise. I can never do anything bad with the small amount of money you let me have.

3

Why should I pretend that men are stronger than I am? We both know that isn't true!

4

— I'm busy doing important things. Don't bother me with menial tasks.
— In that case, if they're so unimportant, I'll stop doing them too. Then I can do something meaningful in my life.
— Then who's going to keep the house clean?
— I don't know. Ask the dog if he has any spare time.

## S·Y·N·O·P·S·I·S

These are the pictures you've seen in this chapter. It will be good speaking practice for you to talk about these pictures once again. Your teacher will ask you "What are they doing?" or "What does this picture mean?" or some other question. You can give a straight answer or you can use your imagination. The purpose is to allow free conversation; there is no "right" answer.

S·Y·N·O·P·S·I·S

5

With a good education, anyone can climb the ladder of success.

7

Being in the military is like riding a rocket to success. I just hope it doesn't blow up while I'm on it.

6

I'm glad my wife and I traded positions. Now I can take it easy.

11

I more than pull my weight around here, but nobody ever appreciates me.

If she ever decides to let go, we'll fall on our butts.

Control your temper!

Not until you control your bad behavior!

20

Why do I feel so out of place in the modern world? At least with saber-toothed tigers I knew what I had to do to survive.

Think of these cartoons as scenes in a movie. The dialog has been scripted. Now we need actors to play the parts.

19

It's harder to lift oneself out of a difficult situation without getting one's feet wet.

18

I wish I could show my emotions freely, like you do.

If you do, I'll knock you cold.

13

It took me hours to apply this makeup. I hope men notice.

I believe the right man will be able to look me in the face and know me for what I am. I don't want to distract him by hiding my true character.

14

I insist on being the subject of my own life's sentence. Not just an object. The adjectives don't matter.

S·y·n·o·p·s·i·s

These are the pictures you've seen in this chapter. It will be good speaking practice for you to talk about these pictures once again. Your teacher will ask you "What are they doing?" or "What does this picture mean?" or some other question. You can give a straight answer or you can use your imagination. The purpose is to allow free conversation; there is no "right" answer.

S·y·n·o·p·s·i·s

15

A good temper means we smile at being kicked. Down with male patronization!

17

I'll support your candidacy as long as I'm sure you're not a two-faced hypocrite.

Don't worry about that. I have more than two faces.

16

In a crowd, all human qualities will manifest themselves — but also in a single woman.

# Murphy's Law

## Pictures Talk

**1** Murphy's Law: You never really learn to swear until you learn to drive.

Q1) Do you sometimes swear while driving? If so, when? If not, why not?

Q2) When you're driving and you swear at somebody, does it relieve your anger or does it just stress you out more?

**2** Murphy's Law: If your condition seems to be getting better, it's probably because your doctor is getting sick.

Q1) Explain why or how that would be the case.

Q2) Do you believe doctors do their best to cure your cold? Why or why not?

**3** Murphy's Law: You check the paper and find that you have all six numbers in the Lotto, but then you find the newspaper misprinted two of the numbers.

Q1) Do you regularly buy lottery tickets? Why or why not?

Q2) What was your biggest prize you've ever gotten? Over all, how much did it cost you to win?

**4** Murphy's Law: Don't worry about what other people are thinking about you. They're too busy worrying over what you're thinking about them.

Q1) Do you care about what others think about you?

Q2) Is it actually important how others think about you? Why or why not?

"Anything that can go wrong, will." That seems to be the only inviolate principle in the universe. I'm sure you can easily recall instances of the principle at work in your own life. Even taking the utmost care is no guaranteed antidote, but nevertheless this seems to be the most effective countermeasure available. But even then, we need to be ever-vigilant. Or else, much to our chagrin, we'll end up calling this chapter "Murpy's Law." And nobody will notice until EVERYBODY does.

**5** Murphy's Law: Everybody lies, but it doesn't matter since nobody listens.

Q1) What's the biggest lie you've ever heard? What's the biggest fib you've ever told?

Q2) How can you tell if somebody's lying?

**6** Murphy's Law: People who love sausage and respect the law should never watch either one being made.

Q1) What would happen if they saw the process by which either item were made?

Q2) Have you ever seen the kitchen of any restaurant? How did you feel?

**7** Murphy's Law: A fine is a tax for doing wrong. A tax is a fine for doing well.

Q1) Have you ever paid a fine? For what? Was it fair?

Q2) Do you think the taxes you currently pay are reasonable? Why or why not?

**8** Murphy's Law: Never get excited about a blind date just because of how it sounds over the phone.

Q1) Do you think a person who sounds lovely on the phone must also look lovely in person? Do you have any experience you can relate on this subject?

Q2) Do you know why so many blind dates are failures?

# Express Yourself Directly

1. Can you imagine why Murphy's Law was formulated in the first place?
2. People who believe in Murphy's Law — are they optimists or pessimists?
3. Do you think Murphy's Law accurately describes a regular situation in real life? Why or why not?
4. Can you make an aphorism of your own that is similar to Murphy's Law? (Such as, "Whenever I wash the car, it rains.")
5. Talk about sayings you strongly believe in as being universally true.

# Let's Talk Funny

## Murphy's Law at Work

A man was constantly disturbed by phone calls while he was in the bathtub. He decided this was all due to Murphy's Law (if he had not been in the tub at the time, no one would have called). But his wife insisted that there was no such thing as Murphy's Law. They made a bet. He stayed in the bathtub all day to test the hypothesis.

**Wife**: So, what happened?

**Man**: You won.

**Wife**: How?

**Man**: You know, I was in the bathtub all day long, and I got three calls.

**Wife**: You got three calls while you were in the tub?

**Man**: No. I got them all while I was out for BREAKFAST, LUNCH, and SUPPER.

## Questions

(1) Who do you think really won? Why?

(2) Can you think of a situation in which Murphy's Law has never operated?

# What Does It Mean?

1

Expenditures rise to meet incomes.

2

I will do it later, later, later, ..

What do you mean?

Delay is the deadliest form of denial.

3

To make an enemy,
do someone a favor.

4

Everything in life is important, important things are simple, simple things are never easy.

5

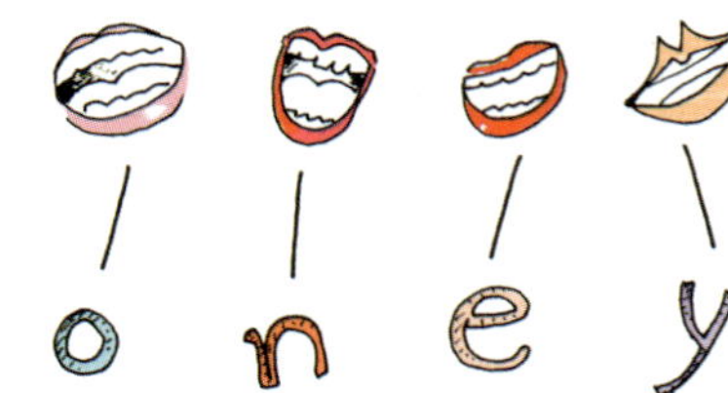


No matter what they're talking about, they're talking about money.

These expressions are related to the topics in this chapter. It will be good speaking practice to let students explain what these sentences mean in their own words in English.

6

If people listened to themselves more often, they would talk less.

7

Arrogance is too often the companion of excellence.

8

Nothing is impossible for the man who doesn't have to do it himself.

9

The length of marriage is inversely proportional to the amount of money spent on the wedding.

10

As the economy gets better, everything else gets worse.

1

Just imagine how mad I'd be behind the wheel of a real car. I need more practice at cursing.

2

The odds against your surviving are more than a billion to one.

10

I'd like to get some burgers to eat, but I'm afraid the moment I step out of the tub the phone will ring.

Think of these cartoons as scenes in a movie. The dialog has been scripted. Now we need actors to play the parts.

9

It makes me sad to see you so happy because I know you have troubles ahead.

When mom takes care of me it just reminds me that someday I'll have to take care of her. No wonder I'm sad.

8

— You sound like such a lovely person on the phone. I'm sure you're as handsome as you sound.
— Yes, when I hear your voice I know you're a beautiful person.
— I hope we can meet in person someday.
— Maybe that isn't such a good idea.

3

I see the lottery ads more often than the Ten Commandments. So I know God intends me to win.

4

That person keeps looking at me and smiling. I must be a wonderful person.

## S·y·n·o·p·s·i·s

These are the pictures you've seen in this chapter. It will be good speaking practice for you to talk about these pictures once again. Your teacher will ask you "What are they doing?" or "What does this picture mean?" or some other question. You can give a straight answer or you can use your imagination. The purpose is to allow free conversation; there is no "right" answer.

S·y·n·o·p·s·i·s

5

I'll love you forever!

He's lying!

He really means he'll love me as long as it takes to count to 4.

6

How was the sausage made?

I assure you that they were born that way.

7

— I'm fair, since I apply to everyone.
— And I'm fair too, since I only impose on violators.
— Together, we are a lovely couple, don't you think?

11

You need to make more money if you want to keep up with me.

It doesn't matter how much I make. You always find something else to spend it on.

12

I will do it later, later, later, ..

What do you mean?

I'm still trying to put off until tomorrow what I should have done yesterday.

20

— Now that I have money, I don't need you anymore.
— It doesn't matter how much money you have, you're still an ingrate.
— When times were hard, we used to get along better.
— That's because we couldn't afford to fight.

Think of these cartoons as scenes in a movie. The dialog has been scripted. Now we need actors to play the parts.

19

I invested everything I had into this wedding. Isn't it wonderful?

You mean you're broke? I want a divorce.

18

It's easy for you to get all A's. You just have to study hard.

How would you know? You're not at my school.

**13**

Now I'm obliged to help her.
I hate being in debt.

**14**

I never expected that going to sleep would be such hard work.

These are the pictures you've seen in this chapter. It will be good speaking practice for you to talk about these pictures once again. Your teacher will ask you "What are they doing?" or "What does this picture mean?" or some other question. You can give a straight answer or you can use your imagination. The purpose is to allow free conversation; there is no "right" answer.


S · Y · N · O · P · S · I · S


**15**

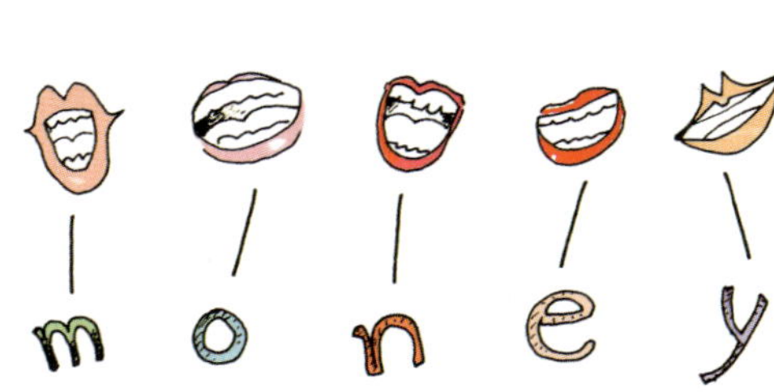


— Marriage
— Old age retirement
— New clothes
— Exciting vacations
— Your health

**17**

Our arrogance is better than your arrogance.

Oh, yeah? Well, our excellence is superior to your excellence.

The arrogant-but-excellents The excellent-but-arrogants

**16**

I know sometimes I don't make any sense but I talk to you all day long. Why don't you ever answer?

My heart tells me to keep still.

# LIS KOREA에서 나온 DISCUSSION TEXTBOOK

**LIS KOREA**는 토론 학습 교재 전문 출판사 입니다.

자유토론을 위한 훈련과정

## Talk Talk Talk (1), (2)

- Express Yourself/Let's talk/What Do You Think?
  과정을 무리없이 이수하기 위한 예비단계로서 자유토론에 대비하기 위한 많은 훈련과정을 포함하고 있다.
- 여러상황에 맞는 다양한 질문을 학생들에게 던짐으로서 질문과 응답들의 패턴을 이해하고 습득케 하고자 했다.
- Express Yourself/Let's talk/What Do You Think?의 주요 훈련 목표중 하나인 어떤 영어 단어나 문장을 토론자 스스로 다시 설명하는 훈련에 중점을 두었다.

토론교재의 베스트셀러

## EXPRESS YOURSELF (1), (2)

- 각권 25개의 이슈와 각 이슈에 대한 다양한 토론주제를 제공하였습니다.
- 토론 주제에 대한 다양한 Opinion Samples를 달아 학습자들에게 도움을 주고자 했습니다.
- 각각의 이슈마다 그와 연관된 Dialogue를 첨부하여 학습자들이 다양한 구어체의 표현을 익히도록 했습니다.

# LIS KOREA에서 나온
# DISCUSSION TEXTBOOK

## LIS KOREA는 토론 학습 교재 전문 출판사 입니다.

청소년을 위한 토론교재

### New Teen Talk (1), (2)

- 청소년 토론교재의 최고 높은 단계의 교재로서 각권 15개의 이슈속에 500개 이상의 토론주제를 제시합니다.
- 각 권에 포함된 9개의 포멧은 (What Does It Mean? / Comprehension/ Teen Talk / Opinion Samples / Dialog / Read& Discuss/ Pictures Talk / What' s Your Advice? /Synopsis/)
  각각의 특징에 맞는 다양하고 흥미로운 토론 주제를 제공합니다.

한국 주제들을 위한 토론교재

### Open to Debate

- 한국 사회에서 이슈화 되고있는 70개의 주제를 선정하여 200개가 넘는 구체적 토론의제를 제공하고 있다.
- 각 이슈의 도입부분에 해당 주제에 대한 다이얼로그를 제공하여 흥미를 더했슴
- 한국사회의 토론이슈를 영어로 살펴볼 수 있는 최적의 교재

# Express Yourself Directly 1

초판 1쇄 인쇄 : 2013년 12월 1일 인쇄
초판 1쇄 발행 : 2013년 12월 5일 발행
지 은 이 : 리스코리아 편집부 & Duane Vorhees
펴 낸 곳 : (도서출판) 리스코리아
펴 낸 이 : 조은예
등 록 : 남양주 제 399-2011-000003호
전 화 : (0502) 423-7947
일러스트레이터 : 김나나
편 집 디 자 인 : 이명금, 전정애
인 쇄 : (주)미광원색

www.liskorea.com